You have To go now
Diane M. Waterman

An inspirational memoir about life lessons
learned in dealing with family addictions,
cancer, death, healing, spiritual connections,
loyalty and love.

Copyright © 2017 by Diane M. Waterman
dianemwaterman@hotmail.com

All rights reserved. No part of this publication may be reproduced, stored in a retrieval system, or transmitted, in any form or by any means, electronic, mechanical, photocopying, recording, or otherwise, without the written prior permission of the publisher.

Dedication

For Mona, Donna and My Family

The night sky is clear and the full moon is a silvery glow. It is big, bright and beautiful in the black sky with heavenly stars twinkling all around it. I always think of my Mom, my Dad, my sisters Mona and Donna and my best friend Beverly who have all passed on in these quiet moments. I think of my baby sister Maye and my only brother Junior who have been lost in their own world of addiction. As I sit on my patio and gaze at the moon's hazy face, I whisper, "Where are you?" My chest squeezes tight and my heart aches. I suddenly feel them next to me and I know they are right here watching it with me, inside my heart forever!

I sometimes think of my daughter Hanna saying to me one dark, wintery morning when she sat at our kitchen table, patiently waiting for her breakfast. Unbeknownst to me, she too was gazing at the moon through our kitchen window, still glowing in the early morning sky. As I stood at the stove, I heard her sweet voice say, "Mommy, the moon is crying." She would have been eight years old back then. I later wrote a song with that title as did a friend of mine. I sometimes believe when I gaze at that face in the dark sky staring back at me, she may have been right, the moon does cry with us when we are sad. What can I say? I come from a family of moon watchers and dreamers.

Acknowledgements

To my children Jason, Jeffrey, Jeanna and Hanna. Each one of you makes everything I do worth the journey. The most important thing in my life that I hope I accomplish, is that each of you are half as proud of me as I am of you. I love you.

To my grandchildren Braiden, Jaiden, Mackenzie and Sofia, may your lives be everything you dream of! Nanny loves you.

To my Mother and Father, my sisters Mona and Donna and my best friend Beverly, I miss you all each and every day. To my sister Maye, I wish you good health and growth in your life and I am sorry no one was there to help you when you were vulnerable. To my brother Junior, I wish you good health and happiness. I am who I am because of the life lessons I have learned from each of you. I am an extension of all of you. I love you all.

To my extended family and friends, who has been a constant source of strength for me, thank you all. I love you. To the doctors, nurses and caregivers who were so kind and compassionate to my sisters, my father, my mother, myself and my family, thank you.

To Loretta Boughton, thank you for being my extra set of eyes. You are truly amazing! I love you.

Steve Harvey has had quite the impact in my life, in more ways than one and in an amazing true story about my connection with him, my twin soul and the afterlife. He has been a positive influence for me in many ways. Thank you Steve Harvey.

To my Steve, you are the spark that lights my flame. Thank you for so many wonderful memories. I love you.

Front cover photo is courtesy of Maxine Gillingham-Patton. Thank you for saving such a precious photo Maxine and for passing it on to me. It brought me back to the time! Cover photo; Diane, Donna and Mona.

Thank you to my daughter Hanna Saunders for taking my back cover photo at my 60th birthday party in Sept. 2016. I will never forget us twirling around the dance floor together.

Thank you to my daughter Jeanna Saunders for taking the photo of me and Steve. It was taken where we first saw each other.

Table of Contents

Prologue ix

1	My Stolen Heart...............................	1
2	Last Goodbye	11
3	Memories.....................................	21
4	Lessons Learned	31
5	My Own Health	39
6	Getting Past "Fear"............................	46
7	The Gift of Giving and Building Self Worth......	53
8	Addiction.....................................	64
9	Happy New Year...............................	84
10	Premonitions..................................	98
11	My Baby Sister................................	104
12	Cancer Hits Home.............................	113
13	Second Time..................................	116
14	Donna's Many Health Issues	122
15	Losing My Soul Mate	131
16	Goodbye Sis...................................	144
17	Messages from Heaven	154
18	Going Back Home	160
19	My Friend Beverly.............................	168
20	Surprise Arrival	172
21	Family Reunion	180

22	The First Signs	185
23	Heartbreaking News	189
24	Middle of the Night	197
25	Criminal Acts	204
26	Dr. Angel	209
27	The Ticking Clock	216
28	Palliative Care	220
29	Painful Fall	228
30	Musical Therapy	235
31	The White Lie	239
32	Her Last Breath	245
33	Goodbye Kiss	254
34	Angels Among Us	257
35	New Beginnings and Steve	259

About Me 274

Prologue

I asked my sister Mona one day a few months before she passed away if I should write a book about our experience together in dealing with her cancer, not knowing if I could or should ever try to take on such a big responsibility and project. We had been through so much by then and the thought had crossed my mind. I made sure I asked her when her mind was clear. She thought about it for a minute and said, "Yes, do it!" We both agreed it might help other people going through some of the same things we were experiencing. I didn't know at the time if I would be able to follow through or not, but I did know, writing about our experiences would certainly help me heal from some of the heartbreaking things we were going through together. This book started out as one of the hardest things I have ever done in my life. In the end, it was one of the most healing things I could have done for myself, and hopefully for others. I was told by an experienced psychic medium since I finished my book that my sister Mona was with me all the time while I wrote about her and that she guided me and was happy with it. I felt her around me when I was writing about her. More than once I looked over my shoulder to see if she was there. That made me happy!

I am writing this book first of all, to honor my two sisters, Mona and Donna. My sisters both suffered from Cancer in their lifetime. I hope to help other families in some small way who might be going through some of the same things as we did in trying to cope with the "Big C" and all of its side effects. My purpose is to not only help the patient, but also the family and friends involved. I also share some of the life lessons I have learned along the way in dealing with many difficult challenges not only in my own life, but in my family's as well. I don't know medical terms, so I will keep it simple. I feel as though I have been pulled to write this book, not really wanting to go back and remember or revisit some of the painful times again. When your subconscious is constantly nagging you to do something, I believe there may be a higher power at work and I needed to pay attention. I hope this book will not only be helpful but also inspirational to some readers who may need it.

Coping with illness and death, seems to be never ending since I reached my early fifties. Losing all of my immediate family in one way or another, has made me realize what I am made of and that I never stop learning about myself, others and survival. To lose my sisters was the hardest for me to accept. I miss them daily! Watching a loved one suffer and slowly die was not something I was expecting to have to do in my lifetime, no one ever does. When you are handed the job of caretaker, it is probably the hardest and most heartbreaking thing you will ever have to do but at the same time, the most rewarding. There were many who helped with my sister Mona's care, and I am grateful to each one of them. After you find you have survived, it can also be very satisfying to know you made a difference for someone you loved, and then you realize there is nothing more important in life than just being there and letting someone feel they are cared for and loved in their final days. Not everyone has that opportunity. Don't be afraid of it, embrace it if you can. If I survived with my health issues, anyone can.

PROLOGUE

I realize not everyone who has dealt with cancer has the same experiences. Every family handles things in their own way, but I believe in many ways, we are all the same in what we go through. We all share victories and the heartbreaks with our families and friends who are inflicted with this disease. There were countless times in writing our story that I would have to push the computer away and literally cover my hands over my face and sob to release some of my pain. I had a lot of fear and anxieties to get past. Going back and having to feel it all, again and again over a two and a half year period, until there was finally some relief was healing for me. Editing is a long process of reliving every word over and over.

I knew I had to be 100% honest and I knew how painful some of it would be. There were a few times I had to leave it for a couple of weeks or months at one point. The stories I tell about myself were sometimes hard to get through as well. I feel good I found the courage to go there. Most of all, I hope my family will be happy with it and be proud of me. That's all anyone really wants in the end.

My first draft of this book took me two months to write and was filled with many negative stories that I feel I needed to write about at the time. I was angry with many family members after Mona died. The more I wrote, the more I healed and the more I forgave! At one point half way through, I left it to God in what to leave in or take out. I was so tormented. If it played on my mind, I removed it. I didn't want my book to be about bashing people I love and there was a fine line I had to watch out for between being honest and not hurting people myself. I hope I accomplished that. I did let a few people read what I wrote about them before I published it and I was happy that they approved. For two people that took courage and for that I am grateful!

I am grateful beyond measure, that I had the privilege to be with Mona and to say goodbye to her before she passed away July 10th, 2013 from Squamous Cell Carcinoma, stage 4 lung cancer. Many will understand who has lost loved ones how important that was to me. She was a tough woman who I became very close to by the end. This would turn out to be not only one of the biggest challenges for my sister, one that she lost in the end, but for me as well. Her strength was incredible and I miss her daily.

I was also privileged to be able to say goodbye to my best friend and soul sister, Beverly Mckinlay before she passed on December 27th, 2010. I loved her dearly, like a sister. She had a smile that would light up any room and I am grateful to have had her in my life for six years. We shared many laughs and tears together. Bev was my rock many times when I needed her and vice versa. I miss her every day. I will always think of her as a shining star.

I had a conversation with my sister Donna, three days before she passed on Dec. 21st, 2008. Her cause of death was complicated, as you will read later. She dealt with cancer three times in her lifetime. Donna was my right arm. She was my soul mate. It was a loss I have healed from but will never get over. She was the one person in my life who truly believed in me and always had my back. We shared an unconditional love and I miss her every day.

Although my Mom was in a coma due to a second brain aneurism, I truly believe she heard everything I whispered to her when I was with her on her last day Dec. 28th, 1992. I loved my mother so much. There wasn't anything I wouldn't do for her and I believe she knew that. I made my peace with her that final day. I whispered in her ear all the things I never got to say to her and needed to. She was everything to me! I love you Mom.

These important women in my life all passed away far too young. My Mom and my sisters all in their fifties and Beverly was only 61. Never in a million years did I expect to lose my mom, my two sisters and my best friend by the time I was 57. Three of them in a five year period and most recently on February 4th, 2016, I lost my Dad. If I had not learned to control my thoughts and stay positive, I would not have survived so many heartbreaks. My family and Bev visit me in my dreams constantly. I love when I wake up and realize I just dreamt of them. Many times they are all there at once. I can't always remember everything from my dreams but I know they were there because I remember glimpses. Other times my dreams are so vivid, I feel we are together in some other dimension. How do we survive these kinds of losses and still recover and go on to live a positive and productive life? I believe in "The Law of Attraction." Learning everything I could about this universal law has taught me everything I need to know to try my best to strive to lead a more positive life no matter what happens. Staying "positive" and "in the moment" is something that takes practice when we have been surrounded by so much negative energy in our lives for so long. Anyone can learn to do this and it can be life changing for anyone who wants to put the work in. It has helped me survive plenty of challenges.

Even after losing my loved ones, I somehow find my way back to being as happy as I can possibly be. I am certain if I had not put so much work and effort into my own healings for many years now, I would not be here to write this book. Even though there is always a sense of sadness that will always be floating just underneath the surface. I keep it there to survive. Most of it simply comes from missing my family. I have always felt like I have been watched over and protected in my life. I don't doubt that I am or I would be locked away by now. I say this with humor, but we all know there is always some truth behind our humor. I enjoy every moment of my life as much as possible. Life is about feeling good in your own skin in every way possible. This is peace!

    My sister Donna was one year younger than me and Mona was ten and a half months older. Less than three years between the three of us. So much of this story will be focused on my two sisters, our struggles, our healings and our special moments together as sisters. The often used quote, "everything happens for a reason," has come into play so many times in my life, but the past few years, it has made more sense to me than ever before. I am hoping by the end that you will know this story was written from a place of love and even the hard stuff is meant to teach. It is a story of great loss, healing, growth, commitment and love. I have changed some of the names for privacy reasons. This is my story....

Chapter One

My Stolen Heart

On December 30th, 2015, I came home at 11:45 p.m. from a night out with friends as I normally did on a Wednesday. I got out of my SUV, walked up to the third floor of my small two bedroom apartment. As I turned to walk in the hallway of my unit, I noticed small chips of wood on the floor and the green mat directly in front of my door had been moved. I felt fear right away and pins and needles ran up my spine! I went to the door and was stunned that it was not locked. I pushed the door gently and it opened. I noticed the wood and door plate on the door frame had been ripped out. As my eyes lifted, inside I could see my T.V sitting on the floor in the hall directly in front of me. There were clothes from my laundry basket and an old purse thrown on the floor with everything dumped out of it. My heart was racing as I looked up to see the light on in my second bedroom, drawers were pulled out of a dresser and more things dumped on the floor. It took a few seconds for everything to register and then the thought that I couldn't deny screamed inside my head, "MY GOD, I'VE BEEN ROBBED!!" My heart sank as I forced myself to turn and run back down to the second floor to the caretaker's apartment. My biggest fear was that the burglars might still be inside my home. I would not go inside by myself!

    Just as I got to the landing on the second floor, I stopped and saw two people coming in the back door. When I stopped, they did as well. They were tenants that were supposed to have been evicted the day before but had not moved out yet. The girl looked at me and said "we are moving." I said, "Okay," and I continued on to get the caretaker. At the time, I didn't pay attention to what the girl's boyfriend (who was standing right behind her with his head hung down) was carrying in his arms. It was much later when I realized it was probably my things in my own pillow slips, in my own laundry basket! I can't say much about those people now, because nothing has been proven to this day, but I feel it was them. My gut told me they ran out the front entrance when they saw me pull up to the back of the building that night. After they knew I came inside to my apartment, they then came in the back door with my things, not thinking I would be running back down the stairs to get the caretaker and might see them.

    When I reached the caretaker's apartment, I was in tears as I banged on her door in a panic. She opened the door and let me in. I explained to her what happened and she told me to call the police right away. She then called her son who lives down the hall from me for our protection. He came to her apartment and after I called the police we all went back up to my place and went inside. I couldn't believe someone had been inside my own private space and had gone through my personal items. I was heartbroken and angry!

    I was walking around taking it all in trying my best not to touch anything. Things had been moved and tossed around with no regard. The neighbour across the hall came out and talked to us, he said he had seen the same woman who lived downstairs outside my apartment door earlier, but the police said later on, they couldn't do anything if the neighbour didn't see them enter or leave my apartment. Really?! The recliner had been moved in my living room so they could pull out a little drawer in my end table. My stereo was gone. My DVD player, basket of movies was gone and the TV would have been gone as well if I had not come home and interrupted them in the act.

When I went into my master bedroom the heartache only got worse. My bed was covered with containers that they had gone through from my closet. My eyes scanned the room and landed on my dresser where my jewelry box had been. It was also placed on my bed. The little drawers were all pulled out and some were left on the dresser. Then I saw the small pewter jewelry box that I kept my sister Donna's ashes in. It was open and the discarded pearls from my jewelry box (which seemed to be of no value to them) were piled up in this little box. I rushed to the dresser and pulled the pearls from the box looking for my sister's ashes that were in a little heart can. They were gone!!!! I quickly scanned the floor, the bed, and there was no sign of them anywhere. I cried out, "THEY STOLE MY SISTER'S ASHES!!" The caretaker hugged me as I cried and I felt my legs go weak. I couldn't believe it! There was more grief to come as we went out into the hallway and I collapsed on a chair by the front entry.

One of the owners of the building had arrived by then. I had no strength to talk and I quickly felt my entire body become pain ridden. The stress from this had already set off my fibromyalgia. I would have spurts of crying and feeling grief over Donna's ashes. As I sat and looked around, I noticed they had opened my granddaughters' birthday card from on top of the microwave, took the money out and discarded the card now sitting on the floor in the kitchen.

We had briefly gone into the second bedroom where drawers had been pulled out of a dresser that contained mostly boxes of photos and Christmas cards. My makeup bag was dumped out on the floor in the spare room. As I sat on the chair and I glanced back into the spare room, it hit me! I said to the caretaker, "please go back into that room and tell me my laptop is still there, sitting on the white table?" My heart raced as she went to check. She came back out and didn't say a word, just hung her head and shook her head "no." Again, the devastation as I covered my face with my hands and cried in anguish. My book that I had worked on for a year was on that computer. Having to take weeks off at a time, because it had been so painful to write the story of my sisters who had both passed. Now it was all gone in a moment, and the people that stole it didn't care what this had done to me. My heart and soul had gone into that book. Now it was all gone with these thieves in the night!!!

I was saving my book "You Have to go Now," on a USB stick, but it had broken a couple weeks before the break in and I had not replaced it yet. I had thrown out the stick, or so I thought. I was not aware at the time, that things could be retrieved from them even when broken sometimes. I have a lot to learn in the technical world! I knew the chances of recovering these items were going to be slim, but I was hopeful I would somehow at least retrieve Donna's ashes, my book and hopefully recover some of the more personal jewelry!

I worked in jewelry for over fifteen years. I am a Certified Diamontologist. Most of the expensive things were given to me as gifts for top sales over the years. Things I had worked hard for. There was a beautiful one carat diamond ring my sister Mona had left me, a one carat ring that I had bought myself, rings and jewelry that belonged to my mother and sisters. Seven watches and eighteen rings had been stolen, plus some earrings. It was the personal items that hurt me the most. My sister's ashes **were** the killer! I felt like I had lost her all over again!

Not only was I dealing with this devastation, but the caretaker's son, who was in his late 20's, 6'3 and about 260 pounds, grabbed me to comfort me for the second time when his mother and the owner went downstairs to find a tool to try and fix my door. He had done it briefly when I was at his mother's earlier and slid his hands down the sides of my breasts to my back. He said he wanted to hug me because I was so upset. Feel me up, was more like it!! I was dumbfounded!! I had chalked it up to maybe I was mistaken the first time. Not the second time. I was so angry I wanted to haul off and hit him!!

"Awwww he said, come here, I'll give you a hug." He was ACTING, compassionate. We had both been standing inside the entrance of my apartment waiting for the police and his mother to come back. This was the guy the caretaker was intrusting to keep us safe?! He took my arms and tried to wrap them around his neck to hug me, I backed off, then he took his hands and quickly slid them all the way down the sides of my body, grazing my breasts and then down to my bottom. I pulled away from him right away and said firmly, "I AM FINE!!!" I was more than annoyed by now. Not only was I robbed, but was I going to be raped as well?! My intuition has been on guard with him ever since. His mother and the owner came back inside as did the two police women who showed up. I put what the caretaker's son had just done to me in the back of my mind and carried on. I thought, "Note taken." I would never trust him alone.

These thieves were anything but smart burglars. They had many traits of drug users, so the police said. They stole some basics that they would not want to waste money on, like, toilet paper. Really?? I couldn't believe that. I had half a pack of toilet paper left in the storage room of a Costco size package of 30 rolls. They even went into my bathroom and took the time to open the cabinet to take the two rolls from there. The only thing they took from my bathroom I might add. I don't have any medications, so I guess toilet paper was the next best thing! (sarcasm) They stole a few bottles of Pepsi, a cheap stereo on a shelf and left two expensive guitars sitting right next to it. I shook my head at these things, but I was very grateful that they weren't too bright.

It was a long night of police coming in and having to wait for forensics to show up, which wasn't until eight the next morning. I had called my children at midnight, but no one had answered their phones. I knew they were all asleep at this hour. After everyone had left, I sat there afraid and feeling very alone. I was not only worried about the people who robbed me but also the man who lived down the hall from me who was after something else. He had said when he left my apartment with his mother, "I will check on you later." I was stunned and didn't know how to respond to him. I quickly said, "I'll be okay!" This was not a good time to mess with me! Sure enough, 3'oclock in the morning, I heard the door close to his apartment down the hall. My heart raced a little. I waited holding my breath and there it was, the knock on my door. I was angrier by now as I opened the door, but I kept the chain lock on. "I was just checking on you, are you okay?" he asked. I replied "YES, I AM, I am trying to sleep!" I was very scared and ticked off! Why is it I felt obliged to be nice, just because it was the caretaker's son?! I shouldn't have even answered the door! I was very stern towards him, trying not to show the real fear that lay underneath.

"Can I come in?" he asked. Again, I said, "NO, I AM FINE!!" and shut the door in his face! I swear, if he tried anything at that point, he would have been the one hurt, because I was one angry woman! That was when I decided to try calling my daughter

Hanna again. Thankfully she answered her phone this time. I told her I had been robbed, and she said "I'll be right there!" She was at my door within 10 minutes.

The last thing I needed right now was to deal with this guy and his mother on top of everything else. I filled my daughter in on everything that happened that night. She was as shocked as I was! I also told one of the owners of my building, Fred, about the occurrence a week later just so someone here knew about the incident with the son. I felt the caretaker's son would leave me alone once he had got the message. He did look scared when I raised my voice and shut the door on him.

After Hanna arrived, we walked around and she absorbed what had been done to her mom. I knew she was very upset that someone had violated me in this way, the robbery and then the caretaker's son. I would want to kill someone if it was my mom. I knew she was staying calm for my sake. I still tear up thinking about it. I could see on her face she was as heartbroken as I was, especially about the personal items being stolen too. I knew she was worried about me and all I had been through in the past years. I didn't want her to worry. I knew I had to show her, I would be okay for her peace of mind. "We will get through this too." I told her.

We settled down after a while, I was sitting in my recliner and Hanna lay on the couch next to me. We had the lights turned out and were silent, both still trying to absorb it all. Hanna suddenly got up off the couch, came and kneeled down in front of my chair and wrapped her arms around me snuggling into my chest. Neither one of us said a word. We just held each other and gently rocked back and forth. This much needed hug lasted for about ten minutes before she went back and lay on the couch. Still silent, we understood each other perfectly. This was deep love and compassion at its finest and I felt it from her. I was grateful for that and I am grateful for her.

We stayed awake until ten o'clock the next morning. I was in severe pain from head to toe. Stress is the worst thing for fibromyalgia and sleep is the medication that helps me the most. I would be sleep deprived for a few weeks after this. Another big loss was my sense of security. It would take time for me to feel somewhat safe again.

In the end, there was an estimated value of 32,000 dollars' worth of items stolen. The insurance had no loss value for my sister's ashes of course, or my book which were the most valuable to me. I had called the police officer who was handling my case five times over the next few weeks and left messages for different reasons, like "I found the photos on my old camera of my things." I had taken photos of my whole apartment years before in case of fire. The police woman had asked me to let her know if I found them. I never heard back from anyone. I went out myself to pawn shops and found nothing. My insurance company would only cover half of what my missing items were worth and they took 30% off the top right away. It was a huge loss for me, especially emotionally.

The day after the robbery, I had mentioned to my oldest daughter Jeanna, that I didn't know how I could start writing my book over. It was 26 chapters at that time and 225 pages. I had it almost finished, without any editing. She said, "You're crazy if you do." I agreed!

I sat alone in my apartment the night after, and twiddled my thumbs, staring out my patio window onto downtown Edmonton and the beautiful skyline. "Now what do I do?" I asked myself in the stillness. There was no TV to watch, because they had stolen the power cord to it, no stereo to listen to, no computer to keep me busy. I looked around my living room to the bookshelf and thought; I need to read a book. Something I had not done for a couple of years, since I started writing my own. I walked over to the shelf and checked out my books. The first one that caught my eye was Steve Harvey's, "Act like a Success, Think like a Success." I definitely knew I had to read a positive book right now and something told me, this was the one. Hanna had given it to me about two years before and I never had the chance to read it. I picked it off the shelf, sat in my recliner and started reading. Within the first two chapters of reading it, I already knew, I was going to rewrite my book.

February the 23rd, almost two months after the robbery and two chapters into my rewrite, I was cleaning my kitchen and decided to clean out my junk drawer. Underneath all the junk, was a little, pink coloured, USB stick! The one I had been using to save my original book on. The one I thought was broken and I had thrown away. When my computer was stolen, I had been devastated about my book, and now as I held the little pink contraption in my hand, there was a glimmer of hope!

I did manage to retrieve my original copy of this book off the stick. I was ECSTATIC!!! It was a great day and I was very grateful. So I have now added the extra two chapters I had already started writing, to the original. I do believe even when something bad happens something good can come from it. As bad as it was in losing some of my personal items, the insurance money allowed me to buy a much needed head stone for my mother and father. It was my final gift to them.

Chapter Two

Last Goodbye

While still reeling from the break-in to my apartment thirty six days earlier, I got an early morning call on February 4th, from my father's superintendent in Gander, NL. The phone woke me up at 7:45am. I answered and the man's voice on the other end said, "Hi Diane this is Harry Martin, your dad's superintendent in his building." My heart started to race.

I said, "Yes?"

"I just went to your dad's apartment and found him very ill. I called an ambulance and they left ten minutes ago to go to the hospital." he said.

I felt my heart ache and I asked nervously, "Is it bad?"

"Yes it is," he replied.

I said "I will call the hospital, thank you" and I hung up, trying my best not to panic.

I found the hospital phone number online and called right away. I knew they would have arrived already because Dad only lived five minutes from the hospital. A man answered the phone. I told him who I was and asked about my father, Eric Waterman. He said, "We are cleaning him up, can you call back in 20 minutes?" I said, "Okay" and hung up.

"Cleaning him up?" My brain and heart was racing, wondering what happened to him and how bad he really was. Maybe he was sick and threw up I thought, trying to convince myself it was not too serious but my instinct was telling me otherwise. I decided to call Aunt Ruby who is my Dad's sister, but there was no answer, so I called Aunt Roz, my mother's sister who also lives in Gander. Aunt Roz answered. I told her what had happened and she said she would go check on him right away. I felt some relief knowing there would be someone with him that he knew and that cared about us. I feared the worse. Dad was very ill and I was too far away to be with him. My need to talk to my father was urgent!!

Just two weeks before this phone call from Harry, I was going through an antique dresser filled with old photos and some old picture frames I had purchased months before from a second hand shop. I went through about 50 photos to find the right ones to fit two of the frames. Finally I decided on two and I placed the one of my grandson Jaiden into the pewter frame and I placed an old 5 x 7 photo of Mom and Dad that I always loved, into the more antique, mossy green colour frame. Right away I remembered the story behind the photo of them when I looked at it. The photo is black and white, taken in 1956, the same year I was born. My mother may have been pregnant with me on the photo; I can't know for sure what month it was taken. When I look back on all the connections to my parents and the significance in this one decision and what was coming, is incredible! In the photo my father is sitting on a chair at the kitchen table with his head down and pencil in hand. He is writing his first song, "My Newfoundland Home." My father told me this many years ago. My mother is standing next to him, looking down at his writing. She is dressed in a form fitting, checked dress with a white turned down collar and white cuffs on the sleeves. Her hair is a shiny brown and is brushed perfectly to the side with a soft wave sitting below her ears. Mom looks very beautiful in the photo wearing black pumps that gave her slender legs a great platform to show them off.

Dad had his guitar sitting next to him on the table and he is wearing dress pants and a golf style shirt. I wondered if they dressed for the photo, but it looks very natural. It is a beautiful and intimate photo and shows her interest at the time, of what my father came to love in the oncoming years, writing and music. This photo was an image for me now of happier times between the two of them.

I placed the photo in the frame and sat it on the end table next to the chair I always sit in. For the next two weeks my father's song, "My Newfoundland Home," was playing in my head from morning till night. It was nonstop! I never had a song play in my head for this long. I mentioned it to two people after the first week. I remember saying to them, "I am worried that something is going to happen to Dad. I can't get his song out of my head." I believe now the photo and his song were my sign that he would soon be going. I kept brushing it off as I often did over the years when I received signs, not wanting to believe it. And now here we were.

I waited 20 minutes then I called the hospital back, again a man answered. I found out later he was the doctor who was taking care of Dad.

"Are you related to him?" he asked.

"Yes, I am his daughter, calling from Alberta," I replied.

"I am sorry" he said. "His sister Ruby Collins is listed as his next of kin. I cannot give you any information."

"Can I speak to him for a moment?" I pleaded.

"He is incoherent." was his reply, "But I will let you speak to Leo."

I was surprised my brother's friend was there, and I said, "Okay." My brother Junior was also living here in Edmonton and our relationship had been very strained. Harry had told me he had already talked to my brother.

Leo spoke into the phone and also told me it was bad. I asked again, "Can I talk to my dad please?" Again, I was told he was not able to talk to me. Then I heard another voice say something in the background. Leo said, "The nurse wants to speak to you." I was getting very upset by then. It was very important to me that I talked to my dad! I didn't know why but if he was on his death bed, this was my last chance to heal some wounds that had come between us since my sister Mona had passed away two and a half years before.

When the nurse took the phone and spoke, I told her that I was Eric's daughter and that I was calling from Alberta. I asked the nurse "Can you please put the phone to my father's ear so I can talk to him?" She responded, "Most definitely!" I could hear the rustling on the other end as she moved the phone to my father's ear. When I thought the phone was on his ear I spoke as clear as I could in my shaky voice, trying my hardest to be strong.

"Dad, it's me Diane." I heard a very light sound and I started to cry.

I sobbed. "Dad, I love you, I love you!"

Then I heard the most gentle, compassionate voice come from the other end. The side of my father I adored.

"I'm okay," he replied weakly. He was near death and was trying to console me.

"I know you will be Dad, I love you!" I cried.

"I love you too." he replied quietly and clearly.

I knew in my heart when I hung up, that would be the last time I ever spoke to my father. I laid my head on my arms at the kitchen table and sobbed. I felt such deep grief and yet I felt so much relief that we got to have that 15 second conversation. It was life changing for me and how I would feel about my dad in the end. It was very healing for me and I am sure my father as well. Aunt Roz told me later that Dad had told her that I had called when she saw him at the emergency room just moments later. She said, "He was very pleased that he spoke to you." Nobody will ever know the peace that gave me.

Ten minutes after I hung up, my phone rang. I picked it up to hear the doctor's voice on the other end. "This is the doctor calling back. We can't get a hold of your Aunt Ruby. We need to give your father blood. His blood count is 'down to his boots.'" Somehow to hear that phrase gave me some kind of comfort of home and it put a smile on my face at a time it probably shouldn't have. "It is 39 and it needs to be at 120." I thought "Oh My God!" I said, "Yes, go ahead!" When I hung up, I prayed, because I knew this was very bad. An aneurysm came to mind right away after hearing Dad lost that much blood. Aunt Ruby had no idea Dad had left her as next of kin in case of emergency. Dad would not have wanted to have any burden placed on her but had no choice. She was the closet to him living there. I don't believe anything could have saved him at that point. Dad had lost way too much blood. Aunt Ruby told me later she was awake and in her room at the time everyone was trying to call her and her phone never rang once. She was upset and confused by this. I believe someone 'her guardian angel' intervened to protect her from seeing her only brother in such a mess.

Not long after, my phone rang again and it was Aunt Roz. She had gone to the hospital and came home briefly to call me. She said "It is bad. Your dad had been alone in his apartment bleeding, no one knew for sure how long." The last person who spoke to him was three days before and he was fine then. I was heartbroken at the thought! She told me she was going to pick up

Aunt Ruby at the senior's home, go back to the hospital, and she would call me when there was news. I was so appreciative that she was doing this and there was still family there who could be there for my father and me. I would have been lost without this contact. I had tried calling Dad on Monday just days before but there was no answer. It was not unusual for my father to turn off his phone and not answer. Junior told me later he had messaged Dad two nights before through email. When he hadn't heard back, Junior called his friend Leo who got Harry the superintendent, to go check on Dad and they found him.

Aunt Roz called me from the hospital not long after and told me my father had gone into cardiac arrest, but they brought him back and they were now taking him to ICU. I thanked her for keeping me informed. It was no more than five minutes later she called back and said his heart stopped when they tried to move him and they were trying to bring him back again. I was devastated by now thinking of what he was going through. We hung up and a couple minutes later my phone rang again and I hesitantly answered, already knowing what my Aunt would tell me. My Aunt's voice was cracking and shaky on the other end. "He's gone!" she said. My heart broke!!!

It was a stomach aneurysm that killed my father. I won't let myself think of how he must have suffered. They figured out in the end he had been bleeding for two days. He is at peace and with my mother and family now and that gives me comfort.

I want to thank Nurse Judy Lush, who has since retired after 46 years of service at the James Paton Memorial Hospital in Gander, for giving me that very special, life changing moment with my dad on the phone. You are now very special to me Judy. I also want to thank my cousin Nurse Karen Blake, for also being there for my father in his last moments, as well as all the other staff and Doctor at the hospital. To my Aunt Roz Blake, Aunt Ruby Collins and to my cousins, Elizabeth, Minnie and Brian who were there, thank you. I know you were all a great comfort for my father as well as his neighbour and friend Harry Martin and to Leo as well. I am so grateful to all of you for being there for Dad and me. I received so many loving phone calls, cards and messages from family and friends. Thank you!

My father, Eric Wilson Waterman, was well known in central Newfoundland, Labrador and beyond. His music was played on radio stations in Europe as well as the U.S. His song, "Sad Day in Gander," is honoured at a military museum in Kentucky, USA, written about a plane crash in Gander in 1985. It was an Arrow Air Douglas DC-8 jetliner, carrying 248 soldiers and 8 crew members back to the US for Christmas.

My father recorded his own music over the span of sixty years, never anyone else's. He was the founder of Newfoundland country music and had recorded twenty albums over the years. Dad never became rich moneywise but he was rich in that he loved what he was doing and I am very proud of him for that reason.

It was about five weeks after my Dad passed that I had a very vivid dream of him. He was driving a black Trans Am and I was with him, sitting in the passenger seat. We had the T bar off and I could feel the warmth from the sun and the wind on my face. We suddenly spun off the road and I woke up. I was happy I finally dreamt of him but what made it even more special was there was a time back in 1983, that my parents were visiting Fort McMurray and my ex and I had just bought a black Trans Am. My Father and I were driving down Abasand hill one day, only he was sitting in the passenger seat and I was driving. I touched the brake and hit black ice. The back of the car spun around and my father reached over, placed his hand on my arm and quietly said, "Stay calm." It kept me calm and when I knew the back tires hit some dirt on the side of the road, I hit the brakes and stopped the car. Dad's reaction and staying calm at that moment probably saved our lives. That memory now makes me smile. To have had that very similar dream with my Dad driving the car was wonderful. I believe our loved ones do visit us in our dreams and I took that dream as a message from my father for me, that everything is okay and to "stay calm." RIP Dad, I love you!

This is a poem I wrote for my Dad four days after he passed:

Dad
My heart is sad, my heart is torn,
yet another love, I have to mourn.
The very man, who brought me here,
has left my life and disappeared.
Though I know you live inside my heart,
for when it's true love, we never part.
Sing loud, sing sweet up in the clouds,
let the angels hear what made us proud.
He kissed me first, the day I arrived,
and gave me true love, that will never die.
I made you happy, I made you sad,
you were my first love, my friend, my Dad.

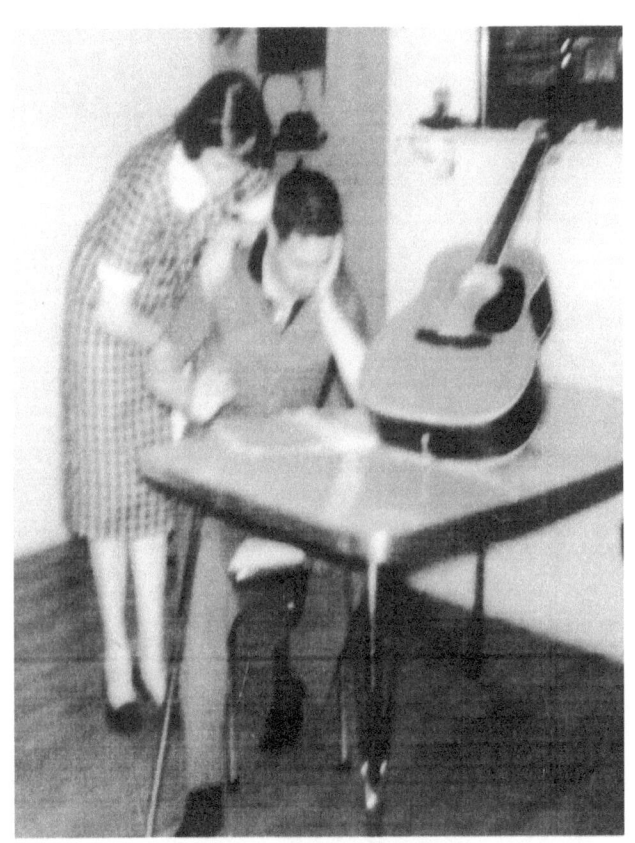
Mom and Dad. 1956

Chapter Three

Memories

My memories of my family go back to when I was two and three years old. My father worked in Gander for Allied Aviation and was transferred to Goose Bay in 1961. He played music at the clubs on the weekends. Dad was the lead singer and played rhythm guitar. Mona was five, I was four, Donna was three and Maye was a baby when we moved there. My family was never rich in material items, but our mother and father worked hard and provided us with everything we ever needed or wanted. Christmas time was celebrated with the usual turkey and all the trimmings, done in Newfoundland style of course. Jigg's Dinner is a meal that consists of vegetables (carrots, potatoes, turnip and cabbage) boiled in a pot with salt beef. Mom always added bread pudding and pease pudding, tied neatly in a cloth sugar bag to add to the pot. We always had poultry with stuffing or roast beef or pork covered with a delicious pastry. It was always served on a Sunday in my family or on special occasions, like Christmas day. When the boiled dinner included the poultry or meat, Newfoundlanders called it a "cooked feed." The smell of it cooking was always inviting and mouthwatering. I still make it for my family on occasion.

Our Christmas tree back when I was a child was always a real tree. It was decorated sparsely when I look at the photos, but Mom did the best she could with a few shiny decorations and sometimes balloons to make it magical to us little ones. It was the most beautiful tree in the world in our eyes. The smell from a real fir tree went unnoticed when I was a child but as I became older and I had my own family, these memories became precious to me. I remember my sisters and me going out with Dad to cut down a tree for the special day when we got a little older. I was around nine years old the first time. We would help Dad hoist it on top of the car and bring it home. The snow would be deep but we would trudge through it following our dad's path, staying close behind him. The soft crunch under our feet brings back memories to me now as to how cold it was, but we didn't care. This was just another adventure with our dad, who we loved and adored. Dad took us on many adventures as young girls and we loved every minute.

It would take some time for us to warm up from the freezing cold when we returned home. We would all take off our snow pants, hooded coats, boots, and our snow encrusted woolen mittens, made by our Grandmother Waterman. They would be laid near the heaters to thaw out and dry. I remember the numbing burn of my red, rosy cheeks and how it would sting a little as the freezing left my face. Sometimes there would be pain in my feet and hands as the cold would leave them slowly. Mom would make us hot chocolate and life was great!

Next we would all have to size up the beautiful, deformed looking tree, and help Dad decide which branches to trim to make it look a little better. Sometimes the tree was too tall to fit in our tiny apartment, so Dad would have to saw the bottom off with his hand saw as we all held it up with our little hands. There would be plenty of needles to sweep up afterwards laying all over the brightly patterned, linoleum floor. When it came time to take it down, the tree would be so dried out by the end of two weeks, no matter how much it was watered, the needles fell like rain. When I would lie quietly in bed at night, I could sometimes hear the soft sound as the needles fell to the floor.

My father would take out his guitar many times and get us to dance in the middle of the kitchen while he played an upbeat tune. Mom would be working hard in the kitchen to make our delicious meals. She was a wonderful cook and housekeeper. She was a perfectionist. I loved to watch Mom and learn. I wanted to do everything just like my mother. I would do just about anything to try and get some kind of positive attention and affection from her. I always wanted to please her and became a bit of a perfectionist myself trying. Although there was never a kind word or affection from her, she was a good Mom and I know she loved us all. Mom worked hard every day to take care of us, both inside and outside the home, so I have accepted those things as her way of showing us love. I loved her so much, I never wanted to leave home as a young woman. Looking back now maybe I thought if I stuck around forever, one day she would give me that much needed hug. I came to realize as an adult, it had nothing to do with me personally but it was simply how she was.

My youth was filled with fun times with my sisters, especially at Christmas. We were four little blond girls who were giggly and always excited to open our presents from Santa. We were sure to get a doll each and coloring books and crayons to share. We all looked so happy in the family photos when we were little. Many times our mother would dress us three older girls the same. Maye was the beautiful baby sister that her older sisters saw as another live baby doll to take care of and to play with. I am sure she loved all the attention we gave her back then. We all loved to play games when we were stuck inside in the winter months. "Little Sally Saucer", "Button, Button", "London Bridge is Falling Down", just to name a few. I don't remember any arguments or fighting between us as children, I just remember the love and laughter.

I loved to read books from an early age and one of my most cherished gifts at Christmas time as I got older was my "Nancy Drew" books. I read anything I could get my hands on and by the time I was pre-teen, I was reading my mother's "True Story" magazines along with the comic books of the time. I was probably a little young to be reading some of those love stories, but I was hooked on reading.

By the time we were in our mid-teens, my father and mother moved us from Happy Valley, Goose Bay, back to Clarke's Head, Newfoundland. We all moved into our great grandmother's old homestead. It was an older salt box home, named that because of its shape. It was a two story home with two bedrooms upstairs, one downstairs and a kitchen. The house was a dark yellow color on the outside. It had no running water, other than a pump at the kitchen sink. There was a well house outside for drinking water. In the summers, the strawberry bushes, raspberries, blueberries, Damson and apple trees bloomed all around the house. Wild roses grew along the path to the well house. My favorite was the lilac trees when they were in full bloom. This setting was my inspiration for the first book I wrote. The smell was intoxicating! There was multi colored wallpaper on all the walls. Mostly flower patterns which my mother changed several times. She also changed the flooring which had patterned, green and red linoleum. There was a beautiful white-beamed ceiling in the kitchen. The house sat alone in a big garden with the river just yards away. I have only the best memories with my three sisters and my brother from that time. My only brother Junior was born when I was ten. It was a treat for us all to have a baby boy in our family and we all cherished him. By the time we moved back to Clarkes Head, I was nearly fifteen and he was just five years old.

When I think back now to how all seven of us lived, ate meals always as a family, watched TV and had our entertainment in that small kitchen for four years is incredible. There were plenty of good laughs and a few tears shed in that beautiful place. There was a table with six chairs and a daybed under the front window. I loved to entertain as a young girl and many times I tortured my siblings, cousins and friends by getting them to sit and watch me sing and dance for them in that small room. The thought of it now makes me chuckle. I was not nervous at all back then as I am now. It is sad how many fears we develop as we get older.

Those days will always be considered some of my happiest years. Our days were filled with exploring our surroundings on the land and the beaches in summertime. In the winters there was always skating on the frozen river underneath the big silvery moon with friends and family.

My father would sing and play his guitar at family gatherings. Our grandfather, Stanley Waterman was a great accordion player and we loved to dance to the uplifting jigs and reels he played. My Aunt Ruby would often play the spoons. She too had a gift for writing songs and poems. Dad's whole family was musically gifted and I have very fond memories of my Grandmother, Minnie Waterman, always humming while she worked in her humble and love filled kitchen. My mother Viola Peckford Waterman's family is also very talented and there still is music being played in their great family gatherings. My Uncle Randy is always the first one to get the party started with his great singing and playing. My mother had 12 siblings and every one of them has a beautiful singing voice and several play instruments.

Music has been a strong bond between my families, all my life. When I was in my late thirties I sang in a band called "Common Thread," along with my sister Donna who sang harmony. There were seven people in the band along with Donna's husband who played the bass. We did that for three years while living in Fort McMurray. It was fun and helped me tremendously with stage fright, something that stopped me from singing as much as I would have liked to over the years. I also sang at the jam sessions at the "Newfoundlanders Club" and the "Royal Canadian Legion" in Fort McMurray for ten years. It was a special time in my life shared with many friends and family. Singing with my sisters and sometimes with my father on stage, was always my favorite thing to do. Although I was always nervous, deep down inside singing has always made me very happy. I stepped through my fears and did it anyways.

Those were the days!

Dad, Mom, Donna, Mona, Diane, and Maye. 1961

Diane. 2017

Chapter Four

Lessons Learned

As much as I loved my father and I have always showed him and my mother great respect, he had another side to him that wasn't as great. My father was human like the rest of us. I feel he had far more good qualities than bad, and I take a lot of pride in inheriting some of his better side. Dad did a lot of fun things with me and my siblings when we were kids. He took us to all the Saturday matinees and bowling. Mom worked in those days on the weekends when Dad was off work. Sometimes she was with us, most times not. Dad took us to all the air shows in Goose Bay. We went for picnics and hikes. Sunday drives with the family and ice cream were always a treat. My father's good side certainly outweighed his bad when it came to being a dad. He could be very gentle, kind and fun. My dad had great compassion for children and animals. I have been blessed with his affectionate and sensitive side, his sense of humor, social skills and creative traits. That was the side most people experienced when they were around him and that part of him was very real. So was the not so likable part of him, which was also very real to me and my family.

    My dad had some anger issues that would escalate, especially when he was drinking. He would throw things or grab my mom on occasion. I have memories of all of us getting in the way of Dad's wrath sometimes. A little fear of your parents discipline is healthy and normal, but this was not healthy. It was something

I became accustomed to later on in my own married life as well. It didn't happen often with my father but enough to make us fear him. If he was drinking, I stayed away from him.

I want my book to be more about the positives of my childhood so I don't have any desire to go back to the details of the scary times but it did affect me and my siblings in that we were very afraid at times as children. I do believe some of it did affect who I eventually chose to marry at the age of 21. It has been proven that children repeat what they have been taught, or else they go totally the opposite as adults. I could write a book on abuse alone, but that is not my purpose in this book. I don't want to go back to all the negativity that I have already put behind me, but I also want to keep it real.

Dad's infidelities also hurt my mother a great deal over the years. He was a handsome man and the women loved him and unfortunately vice versa. That was a 'not so attractive trait' my siblings and I stayed clear of. These truths I had written before dad passed away. I struggled whether I should leave it in or not after he passed. I decided I should leave enough to show that he was human and to understand me a little better and where I came from.

Sadly, after Mona passed in 2013, my relationship with my father quickly went downhill. I tried many times to salvage it. I needed my family that was left more than ever. Dad decided I was going to be the scapegoat for his understandable pain and anger along with other things that were going on behind the scenes. My father and sister Mona lived in that perfect world of denial, me, not so much. Where there are cracks there is light shining through, (Leonard Cohen). I have learned to try and stay in the light as much as possible and still be honest.

My dad being a writer himself, I tried to convince him to write about his feelings after Mona passed. I believe it would have helped him a great deal, but he was so angry I couldn't get through to him. Writing about my emotions and always ending with something positive has been a life changing tool for me. Not everyone will try it. It can be as short as a paragraph. It will help tremendously to get pain and anger out of your system. My dad decided to lash out at me instead and it was very painful!

I decided I wasn't going to be his scapegoat, I had been through enough and I respectfully stood up to him for the first time in my life. Needless to say, it did not go over well. There were a couple of times when he started calling me names and swearing at me over the phone. I would respectfully say, "Dad, I love you but you can't talk to me this way." He would continue with the nastiness and I would say "I love you Dad, we'll talk later, goodbye " and hang up feeling sick to my stomach. I would rather handle him that way. Arguing with him would only make things worse.

This happened a few times after Mona passed away. Dad was angry for a long time after Mom passed as well but not to this degree. Anger is a very real part of grief but never in my life did I think we would end up like this. I thought of the many conversations I had over the phone with Dad in my adult life, after we all moved away from home. They were mostly filled with belly laughs because we shared the same humor, and other times we shared tears after losing loved ones, especially after mom passed away. He was angry at God and he made that clear to everyone.

I knew my father was now at his breaking point, and so was I. I worried about him but I didn't know how to handle him. Being kind and patient with him wasn't working. Dad just wanted to fight with someone and it was me he had chosen to do that with. I wanted to help him but I felt like that fear filled, little child again any time he became angry. Although I had reached out to him on many occasions and tried to mend things between us in the past couple of years, he continued to delete me from his life. From pain comes anger. This was why that last phone call to my Dad was so important for us.

My father praised and complimented me all the time in whatever I chose to do, especially after I divorced my husband and started doing more things for myself. As we got older I always felt he was proud of me and my accomplishments. In those good years, he helped build up my self-esteem that had been lacking. I was and am very grateful for that.

Some of my favorite times in my life with my family were when we would all gather around in our home and tell stories. I especially enjoyed listening to my father's stories. He was a great story teller! He told us many funny stories about his travels while he was involved in the music business. I wish he would have written his own book of his road trips. They were very humorous. He could have us all in stitches with tears running down our cheeks. These are the memories I keep close to me of the man I adored. After losing his two daughters and my mother, my dad was a broken man in his final years. He also had the added stress of being taken advantage of financially which you will read about later. I always tried my best to be a good daughter and I loved him no matter what, and I know he loved me.

I could not write this book without being honest. I believe bad secrets are unhealthy and make people sick in one way or another and unfortunately get passed down to the next generation if they are not healed. I think Dad would have been proud of us helping other families through the gift of writing that he passed onto me. I have to believe that where he is now, he has an open mind and a forgiving heart.

My mother taught me how to cook, clean, work hard, and how to be the best mom I could be in taking care of my own children. She had great wit and she would tell my dad off in a very funny way that he loved. My parents both had great qualities about them that was entertaining to be around as a child.

My mom worked outside the home during the week and most Saturdays for many years. She also worked hard at home, doing the laundry and hanging it outside on the line, sometimes in freezing temperatures. My mother made sure our meals were always made even when she worked outside the home. As we got older, we did a lot of these things for her. I was the curious one that always wanted to learn more. As a young girl I was eager to take on the cooking and daily chores when she was working. I have memories of when we were really young of my mother shearing sheep when we visited our grandparents in Clarke's Head in the summer time. My mother was a tough lady in many ways but there was one thing she could do that I did not desire to imitate. Why she asked me to help her do this every time is beyond me. I say this with humor. Maybe the other girls flat out refused and Mom knew I would never refuse her anything, even if I hated it. After Dad would snare rabbits and bring them home for a meal, Mom would get me to hold the hind legs while she skinned it. I still remember how well my mother knew how to make all the right cuts so she could peel that fur off in one pull like it was nothing. The smell was disgusting to a young girl. She could clean and butcher a rabbit like it was store bought. I certainly did not inherit that tougher side of my mother. I know this is a natural, every day kind of life for many, just not for me. Even though my mother was a great cook and my family enjoyed the baked rabbit, I could never stomach to eat it. It is not necessarily a bad memory for me because it always made me happy that mom wanted me to help her with anything. Mom knew I liked to learn new things, but skinning a rabbit was a bit much for me. Growing up, being the eldest in a family of thirteen children, my mother learned these skills fairly young. My mother was a very beautiful and elegant woman who took great care of herself up until her death when she was 56 years old. She could skin a rabbit and clean fish like a pro. She could also put on a beautiful chiffon dress and look like an elegant princess on the nights she went out with my father. I admired that about her.

    I love my father and my mother very much, and thank them for all they gave my siblings and me. I wouldn't trade either of them for the world. We learn from the good and the bad. I have learned life is as good or bad as we make it! I will always remember all the good memories from my childhood, and there were many. I also don't dwell on the bad, but I won't forget it either. I have to remember, so I don't pass it on. They did the best they could. Remembering the love and good experiences together with my mom, dad and my siblings are the memories I choose to keep close to my heart!

Mom and Dad. 1983

Chapter Five
My Own Health

I feel I must tell you about my own mental and physical health because it has brought me challenges in my life. I had developed "agoraphobia" in my early forties. I had signs of it for years before it became full blown. It is a panic disorder that could be developed from trauma or leading a highly stressful life. I had a few attacks while I was married but I had no idea at that time what it was. I thought I was having a heart attack and I was put in ICU at the hospital at one point. I experienced intense pain in my chest and arm. Not only was I put in ICU but it was the same unit my mother had passed away in the year before. That didn't help me at all. When I told the nurse, she got a doctor and they slipped me a little blue pill. They said it was a muscle relaxer and that was all I remembered until the next day when they did a stress test and said I was fine and could go home. My life had been very stressful for many years but it all seemed normal for me, because it was all I knew up to that point. In 2001, a few years after my divorce, I went into a deep depression. That was when my anxiety peaked. The loneliness was killing me. I needed the touch of another human. I needed love and to love! It was a very different loneliness that I felt than when I was married. I can truthfully say now though, it is better to be alone and lonely than with someone and lonely. Being with someone and lonely can affect our self-esteem in a very negative way.

Some people with this panic disorder "fear" being in places where there is a risk of having a panic attack, others witnessing it and where getting away quickly may be difficult. This is the best description that I have heard of the disorder that describes how I have felt over the years. I wouldn't have been able to put it in those words at the time I was having them and like many; it took a long time to figure it out. It took many years to start to overcome it, and now I know the key is fairly simple. Get over your fear of death! For me, that was the 'aha' moment when I finally started feeling the most relief. If you can find peace with that, you can conquer a lot. I still get depressed once in a while, but I have learned to pull myself out of it fairly quickly and I still get anxious sometimes while driving, but I am 80% better than I was fifteen years ago. If I am in a very stressful situation, I could easily fall back into it again but I fight it and use the tools I have learned. In those situations, I use deep breathing and self-talk to calm myself. Meditation is an excellent tool to learn and practice.

Walking outdoors is an absolute must for me. It has helped me in getting past many stressful times in my life. I fell in love with walking outside back in 1997 and I lost a lot of weight, much of it in walking 30 minutes a day, five days a week. I come to life when I am near trees and flowers. Yoga is also high on my list for living well. It is very calming and does wonders for my aches and pains. The stretching and deep breathing is very good for my body and mind. I started doing yoga five years ago. I bought a DVD and learned the poses that helped my body. I bought a yoga mat and have been doing it at home, twice a week ever since. It has kept me away from a chiropractor for the past five years and is essential for me to stay mobile.

Driving was affected the most for me by my anxiety. Fifteen years ago when I first suffered the deep depression, I suddenly felt panicked in traffic. One time I came close to passing out while driving across a bridge. At the time I didn't know what was happening. There were many times I would suddenly have an overwhelming feeling of wanting to run out of stores. Any line up made me feel like I would faint at any moment. I would break into a sweat and my heart would race. Over a five year period when the disorder was at its worse, I didn't give into the running, not once! Once I started to figure out what was happening to me, common sense told me if I gave into running, I would never stop and I would have these awful attacks forever.

Although I was given no advice on how to even start to get better, other than to take meds that I politely refused, I was determined to learn and beat this disorder myself. At the time I didn't even know there was a name for it. It wasn't until I saw an infomercial on TV late one night describing panic attacks a few years later did I discover the name of what I was feeling. "Agoraphobia" was a disorder I was ready and willing to learn a lot about. I ordered the package and did the program specifically made for people suffering from the panic disorder. It was put together by a lady who had experienced it herself and worked with a medical center and many others who had the same experiences that I did. The more I learned and practiced what the program told me to, the better I felt. There are many programs you can check out online and books to read now that can help anyone suffering from this disorder.

For twenty years now I have fought to stay on top of things and not let anything or anyone drag me down to the bottom, ever again…especially me. I now know only my own thoughts and decisions can do that. I was in an abusive marriage for nearly 20 years and at the end of 10 months of counseling and therapy, I finally found the courage to leave him. It was a huge and scary step for me to take. Those 20 years broke my spirit completely. I have accepted full responsibility for the choices I have made in my life, good and bad. There have been numerous challenges for me to conquer and I have won many of them. My divorce was one of them. Every challenge brought with it a glimmer of true happiness and a new life lesson. I know for any bad day I have, there are many more good days ahead. I love life so much and I don't want to ever give in to a deep depression again. Lying in bed all day long and crying over things I cannot control, is not the life I want. Learning to change my thoughts and how to live my life being more positive has been life changing for me and how I function. In the past ten years, I have worked hard on learning and using every tool I can find to help me live a more positive life.

My belief in God has helped me through some hard times. I have closed my eyes and whispered these three words to myself numerous times when I have been stressed, worried or suffering. "Just Have Faith!" I feel a sudden relief right away. It is a wonderful feeling to know He is there for me always. Learning that whatever I believe will come true has been a very important lesson for me. The two words "I believe" is also very powerful and before we utter them in our minds and out of our mouths, make sure your belief is something positive. Negative brings negative and positive brings positive, without a doubt. People I know who are always speaking of how their life is so horrible will most certainly always have a horrible life. This has been one of the best lessons I have learned in my life and this realization has changed my life tremendously. It makes a difference on how I feel daily, whether I will have a bad day or a good day totally depends on how I perceive everything in my life.

My other health issue that I previously mentioned, Fibromyalgia, has slowed me down physically and sometimes mentally.

I was diagnosed in 2011. It is a disease that affects the nerves in my body and causes pain and twitching in my muscles. It also affects my joints and ligaments. I first began to suffer with this when I was 30 years old with some knee and back pain, but it was never diagnosed properly. I saw chiropractors for fifteen years to help with the constant pain. I have noticed the worst two things that can cause the symptoms to peak is lack of sleep and stress. The pain had become wide spread and worse for me over the past five years that I worked at my job in jewelry. I can only describe it as having a bad toothache throughout your body and adding muscle twitching and tremors. Sometimes there is sharp pain in my toes and fingers depending if I overdo things, like typing too much or walking. There are other times I get a sensation like someone is pinching my skin or a cold or burning sensation, mostly in my legs. It can be debilitating for some and it can be exhausting. I worked for 15 years standing on my feet all day and I ignored the pain and just lived with it. It got to the point where I was hanging onto the railing to pull myself upstairs when I got home after getting off a 9 hour shift. When the flare ups were at their worse, there were days I could hardly get out of bed, feeling like someone had beaten me with a baseball bat. Again, when I am stressed, the pain is worse. Calming myself down with positive self-talk helps. The specialist that diagnosed me said I had to learn my own limits with physical activities. I have to stay active and my body would tell me if I was overdoing things, and it does.

    In August 2014, I started seeing a wonderful acupuncturist Barbara Maddaford, here in Edmonton who has made me feel hopeful about the future and pain control. I had been praying and practically begging my sisters in heaven and to God to help me find some kind of small miracle that could help me control the pain or that there would be a cure. The pain in my body was excruciating at that time. I believe the stress of planning to move back East was taking a toll on my body as well as the grief of losing my sister. Moving was something I really felt I wanted to do after Mona passed away. I felt I needed a change in my life but leaving my children and grandchildren behind was hard to think about. I was torn and it was a huge choice to move but it was not meant to happen, thankfully. I believe now it would have been a big mistake for many reasons. I met Barbara soon after. "Everything happens for a reason."

    Barbara was recommended to me by my former chiropractor when I phoned his office and asked if he could recommend an acupuncturist. This was after calling many places in Edmonton and none of them worked out for one reason or another. I had read articles and watched some videos on YouTube of some pretty amazing work being done with this practice.

    Barbara's knowledge and treatments has been life changing for me. Barbara and I have both agreed, we are kindred spirits. That connection to her was a welcomed and pleasant surprise. We have a lot in common and I have come a long way in every area of my life since meeting this lady. She had also lost a sister to cancer about the same time I lost Mona. Barbara didn't tell me about her sister until I had been seeing her for many months. I was so depressed and in so much pain the first time I saw her, I couldn't get a word out. I was still feeling the effects of it all. I just sat in front of Barbara and cried. I was still totally exhausted one year after Mona had passed. Barbara was so patient and compassionate to me, I will never forget it and I am grateful to have found her. I really believe it was fate, considering I had been packed and ready to move to Newfoundland just one month before. After that trip was suddenly cancelled my life seemed to only get better from there. I walked out of her office after the first treatment feeling like the whole world suddenly lit up. Since that first day, we have had many appointments and she has enriched my life in many ways. It is because of Barbara's encouragement that this book has come about. Months after I started treatments and we had talked many times about me wanting to write this book and my many fears about it, she would say, "do it, I will help you with the anxieties," and she did. She believed writing it would help me in the long run and she was right. I finally found the courage to start it in December, 2014. When I told Barb she was thrilled! She was always very supportive and I felt she was my new found cheerleader. Her treatments have been amazing for me, helping with body pain, sinus problems, allergies, grief, anxiety, and tinnitus. My body reacted well to her treatments. Thank you Barbara, you truly are a blessing in my life. I am forever grateful I met you!

Chapter Six

Getting Past "Fear"

Once we become adults we are responsible for ourselves. Sitting and waiting for someone to come along and take my hand and "save me" was just not realistic but I wanted that for years. I believed I was not capable of making it on my own. I found out we can save ourselves and yes, we all can do it.

It is only our "fears" that stop us from living our best life. Fear is just that, "a thought," nothing more. It is the stories we believe and tell ourselves that cause the fears we have. It is okay to feel the fear but don't let it stop you from going after your dreams. Do it anyways!! The word "fear" itself can't really hurt anyone, it is just a word used to describe a feeling. I believe "that feeling" is the core of agoraphobia (panic attacks). It plays with our minds and we allow it to create the scary world around us by our thoughts. Feeling "fear" when it is our intuition speaking to us is a healthy feeling which we should all pay attention to. If something is telling us this doesn't feel right, pay attention and listen to it. That is our instinct telling us to be careful. There is a big difference in this kind of fear and the fear that we simply conjure up ourselves.

There were people in my lifetime that would mock me when I talked about my dreams. Feeling like the ugly, unlovable child stuck with me for much of my life because of multiple reasons. As children I would dare to say we are more aware and notice everything but don't have the words yet to express ourselves. Keeping my feelings to myself resulted in anytime someone would look at a photo of me and my sisters and ask which one I was, my comment was always, "I am the ugly one." Little things that are unnoticed by adults can leave us with scars we are not even aware of until many years later, if we are lucky. Many people have scars that cause their lives to be dysfunctional and they never figure out or realize why they were acting certain ways or doing certain things that are harmful either to themselves or someone else. Most times adults are innocent in making some careless mistakes and are simply not being aware, because it might be something they are used to. Thankfully, we are all more aware now. By never getting the affection or kind words from my mother definitely had a negative effect on me. My father's anger and temper certainly made me fearful as a child and adult. Being laughed at constantly and bullied for years by my ex made me insecure and his temper also filled me with many fears. All of this also gave me the fuel I needed to prove something to myself, and I have done that, ten times over. I am worthy!!! I know I most defiantly would not have taken the risks that I have or fought for the respect I so desired, without my past and everyone in it. I am now grateful to them all. I feel nothing but respect and love from most people I encounter now and that is a fulfilling feeling. Respecting and loving me first has been key. Change your attitude, change your life!

    My dream now is to help as many people as I can, while I can. Being a good Mom and being a good role model has always been number one in my life. As I became older and overcame some of the old fears, I felt a need to also do more with my life and to place myself high on that list of important people to care for.

Realizing and learning more about this word "fear" has helped me immensely and made me work hard on overcoming some of my own issues and to take many more risks in my life. I have taken plenty of risks that turned out well for me in the end, like walking out of a job with no idea of what I would do next. That led me to one of my passions, writing. Leaving the security of a marriage that paid the bills, not having a degree in anything other than high school and having to be the bread winner for me and my children in my own home was a risk I chose to take. Not knowing where to start was very scary and I also had a very real fear of being killed because of threats. All the stories I had told myself over the years plus all the untruths that were drilled into my brain were all based on "fear." To take the risk and learn that I could not only take care of myself, but my children as well, was a very powerful step for me. Not only that, but to help other people that needed it has been a true awakening for me. That journey alone has been amazing! I soon found out I was not so "unlovable" as I was led to believe. Negative remarks and being brain washed into believing I was no good and I could never survive alone in the world, had kept me in harm's way for far too long. It felt unbelievably great to be free of that! I can't imagine where I would be now if I did not take those first very scary steps nearly 20 years ago to change my life for not only my sake, but for my children and their children and so on. Divorce is not always a bad thing, depending on which side you are on. For me it was very freeing and positive.

Writing not only my first book, but this book, has also caused me to have some fears and anxiety but I am doing it anyway. This kind of fear stops many of us from doing what we are meant to do. I consider myself to be an amateur writer who does not have a lifetime of writing skills behind me. What

GETTING PAST "FEAR"

I am confident in is expressing my heart and my desire to learn. I believe most people connect through the heart more than the technical part of writing. Although I know the technical part is important to learn and can tick off the scholars when it is not done with perfection. (I say this with a grin and great humor.)

This book about family and my own life especially, has been a real challenge. The fear of looking foolish to my family and friends is real. I know there will be criticism from some for sure, but I also know in my heart there will be support from most. Hopefully they will appreciate my honesty. Others won't and that's okay too. The stronger and wiser I become with age the more I am getting to the point that I don't need others approval one way or the other. To get past that fear is liberating to say the least.

Openness and sharing each other's stories freely is how we will all grow and learn. Every now and again when that old voice still creeps back into my head, telling me I am stupid and no good. I repeat my favorite mantra, "Watch me!!!" After every fear I have conquered I hear that negative voice less and less now. Even if I fail when trying something new, I am happy I at least tried. So far the big risks I have taken in my life have all turned out positive.

This is the only way for me to get over fear, walk head on into the things that I fear the most. It is very powerful when you get past it and find out it wasn't nearly as bad as your mind convinced you it would be. I get a natural high from conquering a fear which no drug or drink could ever do. I have fulfilled so many of my dreams so far in my life and I hope I have more to come. Never in a million years would I have believed what I am doing now if someone would have told me I would be writing books 20 years ago. I didn't try writing a song until I was nearly

40. I was so afraid of being criticized. How much I have grown and how much I have healed from so much self-doubt and brain washing.

I will continue to have some fears and challenges I know but I will never quit trying, ever! The challenges I take on win or lose are the rewards for me in my life for the work I have done for myself. 'Believing in me' for the past twenty years has been life changing. Knowing that I can try anything I want and to know and appreciate that just putting myself out there, is a huge success in itself! Learning the only limits any of us have are the limits we put on ourselves! It is a real gift to me, to my children, my grandchildren and so on.

"Fear" can save us, and it can also stop us from being our authentic selves. Always be aware of the difference.

Diane. 2017

Chapter Seven
The Gift of Giving and Building Self Worth

Something very important I have learned for myself and my children over the years is to do service for others. I have watched my children and grandchildren all make me proud countless times with their compassionate hearts. Nothing will bring anyone more joy, happiness and good karma in your lives, than helping others. It is the ultimate gift not only to the recipient, but to you as well.

I have so many stories of all my children making me proud but the one that comes to mind while I am writing this is one of my oldest daughter Jeanna. She is a strong and beautiful woman who has worked hard through her own struggles. She amazes me in her strength and determination in everything she does. Jeanna was going to college four years ago and doing upgrading before she went to university, while raising two girls of her own. As Jeanna was walking outside on her lunch break one afternoon, she noticed an older man who was out in the middle of six lane traffic, looking scared and confused. There were other people on the sidewalks watching this as well. The cars were blowing their horns trying to avoid hitting the man and driving around him. It is crazy busy in downtown Edmonton, especially this time of day. The man looked stressed to Jeanna. She didn't hesitate to walk out in the middle of the traffic and stop all the cars so she could bring this confused man to safety. The man kept trying to pull away, yet he kept saying thank you to her. Jeanna held him there on the sidewalk while they waited for the police. We found out later that the man had been missing and he was an Alzheimer's patient. Was it a crazy thing to do? Maybe, but it speaks volumes of her heart and courage. I know everyone is proud of their children and every parent has proud moments they like to talk about, but not everyone gets to write about them. My kids don't like me bragging about them too much. I do it anyway, that is my right as their mother. My children have shown countless, selfless acts over the years. Hanna has a huge heart as well and thinks nothing of giving to countless people in need on a regular basis. Jason and Jesse are also very compassionate people. Nothing makes me prouder as a mother.

Being rich with material items could never bring me the joy that I have felt over the years of my small accomplishments to make me and my family's lives healthier. Although I have everything I need, nothing too expensive, it is giving to others that has brought me the most joy in my life. I don't know if you can teach people compassion or not but I tried my best as a mom to set the example for loving not only your family and friends but for loving strangers who are in need.

It took me 40 years to finally love myself, and that is not meant to be conceited in any way. It is all about the inside, finding my true self and reclaiming and healing my spirit. My spirit had been demolished and needed a lot of rebuilding. It has taken many years of hard work, being honest with myself and learning a lifetime of lessons to become whole again. Giving from my heart has been the one thing that makes me feel truly happy. I didn't expect when I was 40 years old and finally had all the say in how I lived my life that the more I gave to help people, the more wonderful things fell from the sky for me. It took a few years of small miracles for me to realize that this was what good karma was and how it worked. Learning how it felt to truly give from the heart turned my whole world around because how I felt about myself while helping other people was and is, the best feeling in the world!

I experienced "the gift of giving" when I was young because I always loved doing things for my family and friends even as a child. I loved to see that look of surprise on someone's face when you did something nice for them. It gave me a good feeling. I didn't know, as a kid, the effects and how the "law of attraction" works. Over the past 20 years, I have had thousands of dollars show up when I needed it, numerous times. I even won enough money to get myself a brand new 2012, SUV after 15 years of driving old cars. The tricky part now that I know how good karma works is to remember that when I do good things for others is to make sure I still do it from the heart and never ever expect anything back. That is where we find true happiness. I am certainly no angel, but I know I loved the feeling I received whenever I did something kind for someone else. Being a giving person makes us vulnerable in being taken advantage of as well. Something we need to be aware of and stop if it starts happening to you. There will always be givers and takers. As good as it feels to help people; it can really hurt when people we love take advantage of that kindness.

We are not supposed to talk about the kind things we do for others. Other than my immediate family knowing and maybe a few close friends, I don't share everything we do as a family. I am trying to teach what I have learned about Karma so I will share a few of our experiences.

There are times when my children come up with ideas to help someone. Hanna came to me a few months ago and asked if

I wanted to make some lunch bags and take them around to some of the homeless people here in Edmonton. I was immediately on board and we spent a wonderful day making sandwiches and preparing the lunches. They were received with love and we got to spend a nice day together. This makes me the happiest to be alive. People do these acts of kindness every day all around the world. Some people give all their time to volunteer work and some give millions of dollars to help others. We all do what we can.

My family and I always try to do something at Christmas time as a family to help other families. This is a tradition I want to keep going. Some years I do some small thing on my own. It doesn't have to be huge or expensive. One year my kids and I made gift baskets and gave them to people in a lower income neighborhood. We filled them with toys and candy. Coloring books and crayons are always a hit for any age. There were a couple of kitchen items and chocolates for the adults. My granddaughter Mackenzie did a wonderful job handing them out to neighbors and in the meantime, she was taught the wonderful feeling of giving. Fifteen families were surprised, happy and gracious in receiving them. It made our Christmas! Making cookies and giving them to your neighbors is another great way to give at Christmas time or any time. Volunteer work is always needed and worthwhile. What doesn't feel big to us, can feel huge to someone else.

When I was working for a jewelry company in Fort McMurray just a few years after my divorce was the first time I actually really realized the true joy of giving and the karma affect. I had been saving a little money to hopefully record some of my own music in the future. I had written many songs by then and it had always been a dream of mine to record some of them. Well that never happened but something better did. I had $550 saved

THE GIFT OF GIVING AND BUILDING SELF WORTH

up and it took me about a year or more to save it. I was making about $28,000 a year at the time and was a single Mom, so saving that money took some time. We had a new goldsmith named Neil hired at the store I worked in. He was from South Africa and he was a short, dark, small framed, very grumpy man. He would seem to get annoyed with me more than the other ladies working there but I didn't take it to heart too much. I knew how to handle him. I would be nice to him no matter how miserable he was towards me. I knew his family had not moved here yet and I figured he was under a lot of stress. After his wife and two young children had moved to Fort McMurray, I had met them and loved them. They were very sweet. It was a couple of months later when I heard from a coworker who had been to their home, that they had nothing. They had all been sleeping on the floor and had only bare essentials. My first thought was "how can I help them?!" I remembered the money I had saved right away and I thought about it for a split second and then remembered that friends of mine owned a second hand furniture store. I asked my boss for the goldsmith's address and told him it was for a good thing, not to worry and he gave it to me. I told no one else other than my best friend Barb who worked there what I was now planning. She knew me well and asked what I was up to. This was all decided and planned within minutes. I got home that night and made the phone call to the furniture store. I asked Juanita if I could furnish an apartment for two adults and two children for $550. She said, "They could do it." I said "the furniture has to be clean and it has to be a secret, you can't tell them where it came from." "Alright" she agreed. I just had to let them know the time to deliver it and I did.

The evening of the delivery, I sat in my car and watched the company deliver the furniture. "To give when you have little yourself is always the best gift," and I was feeling the emotional effect of it while I sat there alone watching this take place. It was the most ultimate feeling of pure love I had ever felt. Now I wasn't a homeless person and I did have a job, so I was doing okay from payday to payday but this was all the savings I had. I didn't think twice, and I didn't care that it was gone. Making the CD just didn't seem that important to me anymore. Making sure those children and their parents had a bed to sleep on was. When I got home Juanita called me and said it was done. I told her I had watched from my car. She said the family was very elated, especially the children. The husband was very concerned as to where it came from and kept asking her, getting very upset because she wouldn't tell him. She ended up having to tell him. He said, "You mean Diane from work?" She said, "Yes." She said he and his wife were in tears and he seemed shocked. I felt beyond happy but now I would have to face him the next day and remember, he was not the sweetest person you ever met.

I was standing cleaning some shelves at work when Neil came in the next day. This man who seemed to hate me most days, stood there with a look of bewilderment on his face in the back room and stared out at me with his hands in the air as if asking "why?" I went back and gave him a hug. He said "Why did you do that?"

"Give it to someone else when you don't need it anymore." I replied.

He said, "Thank you." and made the motion with his hand from his heart. It moved me to tears and I had to walk away. The rest of the day anytime I would sit next to him to change a battery in a watch, I could feel him staring at me and he would ask again, "Why did you do that?" I had no answers other than I had heard they had no furniture. He said the delivery people had brought beds, a couch set and table and chairs to them. He said it made his kids very happy. When it was closing time I looked outside the store and there was his wife sitting on a bench and she waved to me. As I was closing the doors to the store, she got up and walked towards me. She took my hands, looked me in the eyes and said, "What you did was big." I shook my head and said "No." She said "Yes, it was big! It changed our lives, thank you." We were both in tears and we hugged each other tight knowing this was a bond and understanding that could never be broken. This feeling was beyond human form, it was spiritual!

It was a gift of giving that I will never forget, not only for them but for myself! I was told by my manager the next day that Neil thought I was rich. He was even more stunned when he found out I was not. I know people give every day and give way more than I could ever imagine, but I was pleased to have made a small difference to someone who had less than I did.

That Christmas I won $2000 for top sales and I received $8000 in tax returns after Christmas. Both were totally unexpected. My ex-husband had still been doing my returns, he had always done them and I let him continue to do them thinking I was saving money. I found out when I decided to go to an income tax filing service there had been many 'mistakes' made in my returns the previous five years. The manager that worked at the tax company said she didn't know how much I would be getting back but it would be substantial. In the end he did me a favor.

This gave me the funds I needed to make the move to Edmonton. I never in a million years expected anything like this to happen to me. I continue the gift of giving and always will, never expecting anything back. The goldsmith and his family became close friends of mine and when his wife got a job at the Fort McMurray hospital and they got on their feet, Neil made me a beautiful ring I saw on a magazine cover and loved. It was priceless to me. It was stolen along with my other jewelry when my home was broken into. The other women I worked with used to tease me that he liked me more than them because he could still be grumpy, but he would become kinder towards me. That is always a good thing. When I moved away and we all said our goodbyes, he said he would never forget me and what I did for them, making the motion from his heart again. The real gift for me was making someone else happy and was worth more than any amount of money. Without realizing it, it was also building my own self-worth. The money was a nice surprise.

    I hope this will inspire others to give from the heart. The rewards of that feeling of unconditional love far outweigh the material items we give or receive. I have been blessed multiple times over! I have been told a few times in my life, that "I am too sensitive" and I agree. The positive in that is I am sensitive to the needs of others. My biggest joy is seeing this gift in my children and grandchildren!

Hanna, Jesse, Jeanna. 1993

*Hanna.
2012*

Jeanna. 2017

Jesse. 2017

Chapter Eight
Addiction

My whole family smoked cigarettes. I had my first one at a friend's house when I was 14 years old. For years my sisters and I snuck them from our parent's packs until we got old enough to buy our own. I have cut back from a pack a day for thirty years to 3 or 4 cigarettes a day for the past three years. I quit twice for three years, only starting up again when there was another crisis. I will never stop trying to quit.

Addiction is a very real part of many families. We all have minor addictions, like chocolate or coffee, but when an addiction is out of control and it is affecting everyone around you, I would call that a major or destructive addiction. It is a disease that has taken its toll on my family in many different ways. I have many family members and some friends who have major addictions. It has definitely taken its toll on me and them throughout the years. I am not an expert by any means but I will share my experiences and opinions about what I have learned. If you have been blessed never to have had any major addictions or have never had to deal with addicts in your lifetime, feel free to skip this chapter, although it could enlighten you if you ever meet someone who is struggling.

The addict will draw you into their nightmare and you can't seem to escape, because you love them. It takes a lot of strength to take "you" out of it. Some addicts will see you living

ADDICTION

out on the street and still hit you up for your last nickel without blinking an eye when they are deep into their addiction. These are people we have loved all our lives. It is hard to always remember that we are dealing with a disease when we are in the middle of it and it becomes hard to remember the person without the addiction.

Addiction has been a big part of my family's life and I don't doubt it will continue until we can all break the cycles for the next generations. My family has always been a work in progress and the key word to healing anything is "acceptance." One of the biggest lessons I have learned in my lifetime about addiction is addicts can only help themselves, when and only when, they accept there is a problem. There are many counselors, programs and centers available now if anyone really wants to work on getting healthy to bring themselves out of the darkness. You have to want it!

Major addictions can rip families apart. The more knowledge we have, the better we can deal with it, but covering it up and lying to ourselves is the worst thing any family or friend can do. I have witnessed this far too often in my own family.

I can forgive my loved ones who have major addictions. It is normal for them to manipulate to feed their addictions, but it doesn't make it okay. No one has to put up with that. It takes a lot of experience to know when this is happening to you, and how to say no to someone who is taking advantage of your heart, because you love them. Believe me; it takes real courage to turn your back on a loved one. This is not easy, especially if you were a "yes" person your whole life like I was. Saying "no" needs to be done sometimes if it means saving you and hopefully it helps the addict save themself. This never means you stop loving them, it just means they have to get out of their own mess and stop taking advantage of family and friends. I will help anyone who is putting the work in. As hard as life might have been for an addict when they were younger, we all make our own choices as adults. I have become somewhat tough when it comes to destructive addiction. I do however have compassion for anyone with the disease and the fact that a lot of people use without even knowing why. It can be very hard on the heart and mind when it is your own family. If you are at a level that is being destructive to you or your friends and family, call a crisis center or family services. They have both been very helpful to me and my family in the past. There is a reason they are there, to help people.

I had known for years that two of my sisters, Mona and Donna, had an addiction to gambling. A few times both sisters had asked me for loans in the beginning of their addiction, but I was never asked often because I would turn it around and ask them questions about it. I said no to them a couple of times. That was hard for me to do, but I could see what was happening. We had all known people who gambled on a regular basis and had lost everything they owned. My family talked about it often. Now my sisters were the ones hooked. After about the third time Mona asked me for "gas money," I asked her if she needed to get help. She looked at me like I had two heads. "Help for what?" she would say, ticked off with me for putting her on the spot. After my sisters were gambling on a regular basis, no one talked about it much amongst the family. Donna fought with her husband many times to quit before she started joining him and eventually they lost their home because of it. I remember clearly how devastated she was. Compulsive gambling can destroy families and it certainly took a toll on theirs.

I know many people gamble once and awhile for fun on a vacation or for a night out with friends, but when it starts to consume your life like it had with my sisters, it was a big problem. I simply knew that when your husband is making five times more a year than I was and they were asking me for money for "gas," there is a major problem. I made $25,000 the first year I worked part time in jewelry. I received minimum child support and no alimony after my divorce. I managed to get by on that so none of this was adding up to me. It would hurt me that my sisters were asking me for money to go and gamble and it made me angry that they got caught up in such a destructive behavior. Donna was honest in saying, "it was a problem in her life," my sister Mona, said "she never had a problem." I was hearing otherwise from many family and friends. It broke my heart and I am sure they both carried great shame because of it. This makes me sad for them both. They were good people with bad addictions. I love them no less for it. I have gambled myself on occasion with friends and I do buy my lottery tickets once a week, but I keep it at a minimum. If you have an addictive personality it is best to stay away from it. If your addiction is running your life and you're not running it, there's a problem.

    I was surrounded by destructive addictions for the past forty four years. I feel I have learned a lot from these experiences. My sister Maye started doing drugs and drinking at the early age of twelve. My sister Donna was addicted to pain killers and both she and Mona were addicted to gambling. My brother abused drugs, my son abused drugs. My father was not a heavy drinker but it would affect his personality sometimes when he did. Some of my nephews and nieces also have serious addictions to alcohol, drugs and gambling, my ex-boyfriend turned out to be a gambling addict and my ex-husband had a problem with alcohol. My whole family's addiction to cigarettes and my own addiction to food have taught me a lot. Sometimes mental health issues not dealt with or properly diagnosed can be the cause of someone trying to self-medicate. Sometimes medications being passed out like candy when they shouldn't be can also be a big problem. I have witnessed this happening too often. Then there is simply making bad choices. Whatever the reasons, we have to keep hope alive for those that need it! We should not judge and look down on addicts and we should not tolerate any abuse or let ourselves be victimized by them either.

I am sharing these stories of me and my immediate family's addictions because I learned the most from those closest to me and I believe they would be open to it to help others. We will be the examples. My sister Donna wouldn't think twice about me writing about her addictions and I believe where Mona is now, she would be open to it as well. My son read what I wrote about him and approved of it. I feel certain Maye would approve and I hope my brother will. They have all grown and are not in denial. There is no shame in courage. We are all here to love each other, learn from each other and grow. If some of us don't speak out and be honest, how could we ever help each other in this world?!

My son Jesse's (his nickname) addiction to drugs taught me the most about drug addiction because he lived with me for one year of the time when he was at his worse. He was using one of the most addicting drugs out there, crack! Jesse has suffered with ADHD (Attention Deficit Hyperactivity Disorder) since he was a young boy but was not properly diagnosed until he was in his early thirties. ADHD is a psychiatric disorder. The characteristics are hyper activity, difficulty in controlling behavior and trouble paying attention for long periods of time. Jesse beat himself up for many years about things he did and tortured himself for not being able to control things he knew were wrong. Having a conscience, he would have a hard time forgiving himself and therefore take it out on himself. He always took responsibility when he messed up and he always apologized. I had no clue what was wrong with him and did my best to deal with it. Especially in his school years when most complaints were that he wouldn't pay attention enough and was too active. Jesse worked from the time he was fourteen years old after school and he was well liked at his first part time job, working at Safeway. He has a very sweet side that people are drawn to. He also has a warped sense of humor and can be a lot of fun. Jesse's twelve year old son has been diagnosed with the same disorder. Thankfully there is more help for people now and we are learning more about this disorder every day. I understand my son more now.

    Jesse is a very handsome, funny, intelligent man who got lost after losing everything that was important to him eight years ago, including his job. He was 31 at the time. Jesse was raising a little girl from the time she was born for three years as his own with his girlfriend and they had split up. He was heartbroken! He adored that little girl and she adores him and still sees him today. His birth son moved away to B.C with his Mom at the same time for two years. That alone made Jesse very depressed. Jesse may be a 6'6 and 275 pound body builder, but he has a soft heart. Jesse then slipped a disk in his lower back while he was at work and couldn't work anymore, therefore lost his job. He was driving a 400 ton haul truck at the time for a company in Fort McMurray. He suffered great pain from that daily. Jesse has been a body builder since he was a young man and had to give that up as well, something that kept him feeling good about himself. He ended up losing everything he owned and then went bankrupt. He had good credit from the time he was a young man and now that was also ruined. To deal with his ADHD and try and handle all of this was a lot! Jesse went into a downward spiral and a deep depression. He eventually moved from Fort McMurray to Edmonton. I let him live with me to help him through a very tough time. What I didn't know at the time is that my son had started using crack and he had been introduced to it by my brother. My son admitted later he had been using cocaine for a while before my brother asked my son at his lowest, to try the crack. My son turned it down the first time, but not the second. There are no words for how I felt when I found this out. The hardest part of dealing with Jesse's ADHD and his addiction was his attempts of suicide. How could I be strong and tough with my son who so desperately fought to get better, but would then try and kill himself?! I had to figure it out by instinct alone.

I had no idea what was going on at the beginning, it was all new to me. After two years of hell for me and my family, I had learned a lot about "destructive addiction." I learned enough that I would no longer be Jesse's enabler. It was so bad at one point I came home from work one day to find my son lying on the floor in my hallway, overdosed and dying. I shook him and called out his name a few times with no response but I could tell he was still breathing. I grabbed the phone and called for an ambulance. The dispatcher told me to calm down or they would be sending an ambulance for me. I was panicked and heartbroken!! The ambulance came and thankfully he was saved. He was kept in the hospital for two days and then they released him. I was so upset I phoned the head psychiatrist at the hospital and asked why he was released. They had no choice he said, he released himself. I had no help whatsoever.

My son tried killing himself several times that year but I won't give all the details, we are past all that now. It was a clear cry for help and a mother's worst nightmare. I tried everything I could to help him in those two years and then one day I realized

I wasn't helping at all. I was enabling him, constantly! That had to stop! Jesse had to save himself. I don't know how I have always figured these things out myself other than watching people, learning behaviors and patterns, figuring them out and common sense is important. I had watched many programs about addiction over the years and I had learned enabling is the worst thing anyone can do for an addict. Dealing with a "suicidal addict" was a nightmare and torture for me as a mother. I couldn't bear the thought of losing my son and I wanted to save him, hence came the enabling. Some things we don't need a degree in psychology to figure out. Some people with the biggest degrees have no common sense. I was still learning!

Jesse moved out eventually and moved in with his sister when he had stopped using for a short time. That didn't work out because he kept relapsing back into the drug world. He wanted to move back in with me at one point when his sister had enough and he had nowhere else to go. I would give the world for my children like most mothers would, but I had learned my lesson about enabling, and turned him down flat! That took more courage than anyone will ever know, especially when your adult child is near death, out on the street and asking to live with you again. I had already done everything in my power to try and save him including spending most of my savings over two years, which was close to $14,000 at this time. It was now up to him to save himself. It was a very scary time! I had to muster up all the faith I had in me and believe in my son.

After two years, I had tolerated being harassed at home and at work long enough. My son had turned into someone I no longer recognized. His addiction was ruining our relationship on every level. It was time to be tough if there was any chance left of my son being saved. I wanted my son to be well and I would fight for him, but at a distance. I had to protect myself at this point or I would be out on the street as well. I felt at the time Jesse was going to die either way. If I didn't be strong and say "no" to him, as scary as it was, he would surely die from an overdose or worse, which I would have paid for. And if he died, so would I! I had to take the risk that he would survive and get better, depending on my own strength. I firmly said "NO" to him with no explanation. I then prayed a lot and passed it over to God. It was a battle at first when I turned him down. He didn't want to take no for an answer and he used all the usual guilt trip lines he had up his sleeve on me. I stood firm! That was the day he finally went into detox, then sober living for the next two years. To watch my son admit and accept his issues and fight to get healthy has made me proud beyond any words I could ever express!

    I had written a note and placed it in an envelope I had dropped off to him one day while he was in detox. I asked for him to ask the people in detox to please put him in sober living. I said, "Beg for it if you have to." Jesse had been in detox a few times before but made many excuses why he couldn't get into sober living. I also repeatedly made it clear to him that he could not live with me anymore once he got out of detox and I would not give him money! He finally asked for the help he needed and after six years, with a few relapses under his belt, he has stayed firm and strong to fight this disease and is thriving today because of his sheer will and determination. My son now has the tools he has learned to help him. I am very proud of him and the work he has done. He is in a good place now with a good job and his own place. He thanked me in a letter when he was in sober living, for being strong. He wrote "you saved my life." I believe he saved his own life in the end. I also had to believe he would be okay and he was. My son is a wonderful writer and has become very good at expressing himself and helping others. He took responsibility and apologized for the harm he caused. He has a big heart and I hope one day he will write his own story that can help others survive. Jesse is my inspiration!

My brother Junior has also struggled with addiction for a very long time. My relationship with my brother is of course different than the one with my son. I don't know the reasons my brother started using in the beginning. I do know he was playing drums in a band at the time and someone offered crack to him and he tried it. He had a good life going for himself at the time and it fell apart soon after that. My brother is not a bad guy either. I don't know of him ever getting in trouble with the law or anything crazy.

My sisters and I kept it quiet from Dad for some time at the beginning that our brother was using crack. Mona was the first to find out and wanted us to be quiet about it, not to upset Dad. My brother had admitted it to her over the phone one night fourteen years ago in a tearful conversation, that he was using crack. Keeping it from our father was her way but not mine. One day when I heard about all the money our father was sending my brother I said, "I am telling Dad the truth" and I did tell him. I felt Dad had a right to know where his money was going. I wish someone would have told me the first year my son was using. I was clueless about the drug at the time and the lies I was being told to get money out of me were endless.

As much as I tried, I couldn't convince my father that he was being lied to and used for drug money by my brother and that caused a lot of friction between the three of us, especially the last few years of my father's life. I had learned a lot about the tricks of the addict by then. Dad only had a pension to live off. He was giving his money to Junior constantly. This had been going on for much of fourteen or fifteen years. My father admittedly said, he had given my brother close to $50,000 over that time span. My brother admitted that to me as well. Crack is an expensive drug. I have several family members and friends who have spent that much and more on gambling addictions. The strain on the finances of families dealing with these major addictions is tremendous and stressful for everyone involved. It can ruin families! Saying 'NO' without any explanation is okay and necessary. Say it a hundred times if you have to because most addicts don't give up easy.

So many families have gone through the same things but not all will be honest about it or want to admit it. Considering my father was not a rich man at all, that was a lot of money. Dad would call me sometimes frustrated and not knowing what to do because my brother constantly needed money from him, even when he was working and making good money himself. There were times when my dad would say he wasn't giving him any more money but it didn't last long. Addicts will come up with a crisis to suck us (their enablers) in to handing out money to them. I was looking out for my dad.

One of the things many major addicts are good at doing is complaining about what they don't have, money for food and so on, playing on their loved ones emotions until we give them what they want so they can feed their addiction. That way they can say, "I never asked for anything." That is asking, but being manipulative about it. "Poor me" works for a while and most major addicts use it. I don't mean you should never have any compassion; it is a disease after all, but you can buy them food instead of handing over money. Limit your involvement with enabling them. Sometimes we have to cut them off completely for their sake and ours. Major addicts will cling on to the one person they think they can get the most out of and clean that person out completely, if we let them.

My brother knew he could play my dad and make him feel sorry for him, and he did. No different than how my son played me for two years. This was fourteen years later and it was still going on with my father and brother. As parents we naturally want to help our children no matter what age they are, so it is tough to say no, especially when they are getting us to feel sorry for them. I am protective and motherly by nature. I was a big problem for my brother in trying to protect my father. I was getting in the way of his cash flow. That did not go over well. The addict who is in denial will always play themselves as the victim.

Junior never showed up a lot, which also caused a lot of mistrust between us. This seems to be another familiar trait of major addicts. The last two times I reached out to Junior there was no response, which is normal for him. My sister Maye does the same. They disappear until you hear from them again. Many months went by again before I finally did speak to Junior. Unless you are the one feeding the addicts addiction, it is normal not to hear from them when they are deep into it. I try not to take it personally and I always tell my brother I love him after every conversation if he does reach out to me and he tells me the same. What has hurt me the most in this case was not only how his addiction came between me and him, but how it came between me and my father. It can rip families apart.

"Where will he go to live if he loses his apartment?" my father asked me one day over the phone while Mona was sick. "There are shelters here and sober living if he wants to go there," I answered. Dad was surprised by my response and expecting me to say I would take care of Junior. I was not so soft anymore and I had learned many lessons by then. I also felt I had enough to worry about with Mona being so ill at the time. My father had not been around all the addiction that I had been for years and he did not understand it, so I forgive him for that. It takes time and experience for someone to clue in to what's going on around us because we are being lied to constantly by the addict. Taking care of Mona was enough and to now put more pressure on me to take care of my brothers needs as well was overwhelming for me to say the least.

On rare occasions some addicts seem to be honest with themselves and others, that they have issues. They take responsibility for their actions without making the excuses or blaming others. That is a healthy start to recovery and shows their integrity is still intact.

Addicts carry tremendous shame, which is a shame because all their loved ones ever want for them is to be healthy and happy. Just because someone has flaws we don't stop loving them. We can help others by sharing what we know and that is my purpose here. I hope my brother understands that. I really want him to be healthy and I believe he can be. He does try harder to stay in recovery now and I pray every night that he succeeds. I would love nothing more than to have a healthy relationship with my brother. I love him and miss his big bear hugs. I know he carries his own pain and I pray he heals himself. I hope someone else may take something from our story and can use it in a positive way to help themselves or a family member or friend in crisis.

Destructive addictions can change a family's dynamics. The focus is inevitably always on the addict in the family when they are using. Worry, worry, worry! Sometimes we as parents or family and friends have to step out of the picture for the sake of ourselves, the addict and the rest of the family that deserves some positive attention. Never give up on the family member struggling.

ADDICTION

Sometimes we just have to do it at a distance. Sometimes addicts take their own lives. None of us have control of another person and that is the saddest ending that could happen to any family.

Most days with my mom, dad and my two sisters who have passed on and having little to no contact with my only two living siblings, for months and years at a time depending on where they are in their addictions, I feel I am pretty much alone in the world. If it weren't for my children and grandchildren over these past years, I would feel more alone than I could ever possibly bear.

Where Junior shines the most is playing the drums. My father and I both agreed my brother is one of the best drummers we have ever heard, and we have heard many. I would rank him up there with Phil Collins, one of my brother's idols. I may be partial because he is my brother but his timing is impeccable. I pray one day he will get back to enjoying his passion and living the good life he deserves!

I am far from perfect but I am honest, especially about myself. I struggled with food addiction most of my life. It was my drug of choice. Food filled the deep hole in my heart for many years. I was emotionally starved and depressed for a lot of my marriage. The food gave me some kind of relief and comfort from the pain I was in. Not much different than why people abuse gambling, drugs, alcohol and so on. The person I was hurting the most was me by abusing my body with this unhealthy life style. I painted on a smile most days for my family and friends but I am certain they sometimes saw through it. What saddens me the most is how it may have affected my children. I am sure having a mom who was depressed sometimes and couldn't do a lot of physical things with them that I might have if I was fit, was not easy for them either.

The sugar highs temporarily filled up that deep hole in my heart of never feeling loved. I felt stuck in the middle of something that was anything but loving. Getting control of my food addiction was life changing for me in how I looked and felt about myself. With ten months of therapy and many years of practicing positive mantras daily, believing in myself, giving to others and using everything positive I could read and learn from, I feel I am doing well. Building my self-worth is a continuous job that I wake up feeling determined to work at every day. The "never give up" attitude has kept me alive and got me through a lot of pain in my life, both mentally and physically.

I have kept junk food under control for most of 20 years now. Seeing a therapist twenty years ago and exploring what was 'eating at me' was crucial and healing. To lose weight I figured things out as I went along. I learned to eat as healthy as I can. I have many food sensitivities so I can't eat as many fruit and vegetables as I would like. I quit eating deep fried foods and kept the sugar under control. I still have a little bite if I need it. I learned that cutting myself off completely from my cravings would only make me binge eat and go off my diets. I have my piece of chocolate every day but I never eat a whole chocolate bar. There was a time I could eat two or three in a day.

I lost 100 pounds around the time of my divorce and have pretty much kept it off. Before that I did many years of yoyo dieting, eating my way through the depression of being in a marriage I was very unhappy in. When Mona was sick, I did gain back 40 pounds. My diet was the same but I have always had a very low metabolism, so exercise is crucial to me and I wasn't doing any exercise at that time. I was sitting with my sister daily for many months and it caught up to me. It was my fault for not making the effort. I have since lost it again after a year of walking, yoga and staying as active as I can while living with fibromyalgia. Anyone having this disease knows we have our limits.

I really don't like the word diet but that's what everyone called it in the eighties and nineties. I simply live a healthier life style now. To feel good takes work and it is important to stay focused on the day you're in and don't worry about the future when trying to lose weight. Any time your mind starts to wonder into the future of how long you give yourself to lose a certain amount of weight, pull yourself back to focus on the day you are in! That was the biggest thing I learned after many years of trying to lose weight and failing. Stay in the day!!! I believe that is crucial for any addiction. Anytime your mind starts to wonder to things like 'I have to get fifty pounds off for the wedding in six months' STOP yourself and bring yourself back to the moment and day you are in! Your mind will wonder a lot in the beginning because we love to plan everything and try and control the future. Believe me I did this a thousand times over the years. This kind of thinking will throw you off. Stay in the day and stay focused! Trust me, it works! I also stopped weighing myself. I got on the scales one time in a year when I lost the hundred pounds. Many years of experience before that had taught me that weighing myself weekly would only frustrate me when I had weeks that weren't so great and I would turn to junk food again whenever I was not losing as much as I thought I should have been. Everyone is different, but staying off the scales worked for me.

How does someone with a soft heart survive a lot of drama without a partner to lean on? It is not easy! There were countless times as a young girl and woman when my feelings were hurt or when I was being abused, that I would cry out for my mother in my head, holding everything inside and eating my pain away. That need to be held and feel safe in the world never really goes away but the crying out for someone to save me did go away when I found my own strength and healing. Maybe I also cried out for my mother because that affection I so needed from her was missing for me my whole life. The affection I so easily share with my own children and grandchildren.

No one would judge honesty, at least I wouldn't. I admire the people that will own it and not lie to themselves and the people around them. That takes a lot of courage. It means that person not only values their loved ones, but more importantly, they value themselves and it is often the first step to getting well. I remember many times the feelings of desperation when I felt no way out of a bad marriage and suffered with an eating disorder. There is help out there if anyone wants it. I am not an expert by any means. I only speak from my own experience and what has worked for me and my family. It is important to me to break some of the unhealthy patterns I lived with for the next generations, by putting a lot of work into my own healing over the past years.

My adult children have proven to me in many ways that they are all much healthier already than I ever was. When they have had problems, if they can't solve it themselves they seek help. My daughter Jeanna gained a lot of weight after having her two daughters and she has also lost 100 pounds and is keeping it off. I am very proud of her; I know how hard that is to accomplish. My kids not only take care of their physical health but their mental health as well. We have all went to therapy when needed. I think most of us need a certain amount of therapy. It is good for the soul. My kids all go to the gym, they don't smoke and they all eat very healthy. I am very proud of them all for having that courage and will power to lead a healthy life style. They still love a home cooked meal once in a while at Mom's house and I do keep cookies on hand for their visits. We all have a sweet tooth; we just have to keep it under control.

Marrying who I had married was a blessing in some ways and I wouldn't change it, because I have three beautiful adult children and four wonderful grandchildren from it. It was not all bad. I did love my ex for nearly 20 years, as unhealthy as it was. I do wish good things for him. I know he has a past like most of us and hopefully he has healed himself.

The past seven years have been some of the toughest years I have been through and I had survived a lot from before then. Losing my family and dealing with all the family addictions, was far beyond what I thought I would have to take on in my later years. How I had not turned to more destructive behaviors myself is beyond me. I do know I have a strong will and do want to be the best example for my children and grandchildren. That has always been my main focus.

Most people who are caught up in addiction are good people. We need to break the cycles of destruction in families by being strong and being the positive examples, getting the help we need when we need it. It takes great determination to make a positive change and anyone can do it!

The more we survive, the stronger we become. I see survivors as oak trees that after weathering hundreds of storms only become stronger and more resilient with age. Where do we find that strength to go on and not fall into something bad for us to ease our pain, especially after the death of a loved one? Personally, I loved therapy when I went twenty years ago. I also write to help sort out my feelings and I am a talker. It is not healthy to keep pain buried. We should all know that by now. Addiction can sneak up on you, making bad choices in times of pain. There are other times, like you will read about my sister Donna, that there was no choice but to use an addictive drug.

Opening your heart and soul to truth can be scary for many of us because then we no longer have an excuse to stay broken and depend on addiction and others to fix it. We have to fix it ourselves. It is much easier to stay broken and live a hopeless life of darkness than to put the work in to be healthy. Only the courageous will win that battle! That is a powerful thing when it happens for any of us and that kind of strength comes with acceptance, willpower and a strong determination to be happy and healthy, one day at a time!

Thankfully I love to read and reading is knowledge. Life is wisdom, and I love to learn. I help myself through learning, writing and sharing my own pain. Taking control of every aspect of my life after being controlled for so many years has been a thrilling journey for me and I wouldn't trade it for anything.

Sometimes when we don't feel mentally and physically strong but everyone around us believes and says we are, I wonder if maybe that's what keeps us strong, people telling us we are? I think it does help tremendously and I thank my family and friends for telling me that often.

Deep down inside I just want to RUN as far away as I could possibly go when there is yet another crisis to deal with. I know there are a lot of people just like me who need support in some way. I have many family and friends on social media that have helped me tremendously through some dark times. I pray a lot and I have learned to pass it over to God when the challenges get too big for me to handle alone. Prayer has been my saving grace. I am learning to do that more and more as my faith becomes even deeper. I seem to somehow bounce back after every battle that has tortured my heart and soul, thinking numerous times, "I will be amazed if I survive this one!"

It is up to us to seek help when there has been abuse, addiction or other family dysfunctions. We all have to take responsibility for our own mental and physical health, unless it is an illness that leaves a person powerless, and do the work to have a better life. Suicide is never the answer, even in times of desperation. Reach out for help! I believe suicide is the most painful death for any family to deal with. I always think of the mother first when I hear of another suicide, no matter what age, my heart aches for them. Tell someone you trust if you are carrying a burden, no matter how big or small you think it may be. Calling a hotline or crisis center can be the first step for many who are desperate. They will steer you in the right direction. The people working there are amazing and helpful.

For every negative, there is a positive. It is up to us to find as many positives to help us as we can. One of them is learning!

Chapter Nine

Happy New Year

At the tender age of 18, I became pregnant. I had a baby boy nine months later. I felt at the time that I had no choice but to put him up for adoption when I wanted nothing more than to keep him. The choice I felt I had to make literally broke my heart! Jason's birth father walked away after I told him I was pregnant. He did speak to me one time a few weeks after I gave birth. I had only slept with Jason's birth father twice. I believe I became pregnant the first time. Tim had pursued me from the time I was fifteen. On my eighteenth birthday was the first time he had wanted sex and I said "yes." I asked him to use protection and he did but then removed it. I blamed myself and carried the guilt for years to come because I said nothing. I was in my early thirties before it hit me why he never pushed me more to go further before my eighteenth birthday. I again, was a naive teenager. Tim was six years older than me and I thought I loved him as any teenager could love. We were both responsible for what we did but I certainly carried enough guilt and shame for both of us. Now that I am more than four decades older I see things much more clearly. My eighteenth birthday was September 25, 1974 and Jason was born on June 25, 1975. He is a blessing, he was never a mistake!

The nine months of being pregnant was a very long and lonely time for me. When Jason's birth father stepped out of the picture and I was left tortured on making a choice in what I should do when the baby came. I kept it from my parents for as long as I could, afraid to tell them. They had been through so much with my sister Donna being sick with cancer and I had witnessed my father's reaction when Mona became pregnant with her first child. I was scared and felt very alone. There were so many things I had to consider. I was clueless on how to take care of a new born baby by myself and I felt pressured to give him up once my parents did know. No one was offering to help me in any way and being the person that I am, I would never ask for any help. I know now those feelings came from not feeling worthy. I felt it was very much my own fault that I was in this situation and I would be the one that had to make the final choice. Jason's birth father made no attempt to see me or talk to me. It wasn't until the day I delivered Jason, that I did make the final decision to put him up for adoption. My soul was tortured! In the end, I wanted to do what I thought was best for my child and I had to put my own feelings aside. I also felt I had no other options. I felt helpless! I did know I wanted him to have a stable home with two parents. I was heartbroken with the decision, so depressed in my bed on the hospital ward after the birth of my son, that one of the patients went to a nurse and asked her to keep an eye on me. I remember that nurse coming to talk to me and how sweet she was. I felt my heart and soul had been ripped from my body, and it was!

    I never got to hold my son or see him. I just saw his tiny feet when he was born. I was told by the social worker I would not be allowed to see him and I think it was the only way I went through with it. Back at that time it was normal to spend at least five days in the hospital. It was torturous for me to lay there for those days knowing my son was down the hall from me and I couldn't see him or hold him. He was all I thought about. Other than telling my ex-husband when I met him and my youngest son when he was eight, I never spoke of it to anyone else from that day on. Although my family and friends were all aware of it, I just couldn't talk about it. I buried it deep, for fifteen years. When it finally came up in a therapy group fifteen years later, I found out how much pain I had really buried for all that time. After I had my last child Hanna in 1990, I suffered with Post-partum depression. I didn't know what was wrong at the time and two weeks after I had her I called a help line because I felt suicidal. It was suggested to me to see a therapist who then signed me up for a therapy program. My sister Donna went with me. It was at a group session that the adoption finally came up. It felt like my chest was going to crack wide open before I fell completely apart. Donna said afterwards, "It was like listening to a wounded animal." My cries were an uncontrollable howling from somewhere deep that I didn't even know existed. Then the silent tears, the sadness went on for many days after. To finally release it all back in 1990 was very freeing for me and I could suddenly breathe deeper but still my heart ached for him and that longing to know him and hold him, never went away.

We don't realize what we carry around inside until we go to speak of something painful. That's when we really find out how much we bury. The guilt of what I did carried an even bigger burden for me. As painful as it was to finally talk about everything fifteen, long years later, it got easier for me the more I did finally start to share with my sisters. More than my own pain, I regretted the pain I knew I caused my son. Jason has never made me feel guilty for the decision I made in 1975. He is an awesome young man who after almost 25 years, I finally got to meet. He is 41 now. I feel very grateful and blessed to have him in my life in any way. The way we first met was incredible in itself.

On December 31st, 1999, I made my first connection ever with a psychic. A neighbor of mine told me about a number he had called and had an incredible reading. I wasn't going out anywhere for New Year's, which was normal for me, so I thought, why not entertain and treat myself on New Year's Eve?!

I did what my friend told me. I had a paper and pen in hand so I could take notes. I was anxious never having done anything like this before. I had been living on my own for more than two years then and was more than ready to find a new love. That was the reason for the call. I wanted to know if there would be anyone new in my future in a romantic way. I was very lonely, something I would adjust to over a twenty year span. I always did believe there were physics with gifts, because I had experienced so many spiritual things myself.

I thought of Jason all the time and especially on special occasions like Christmas and his birthday, but never in a million years did I dream he would come up in this reading. Jason would have been 24 years old at the time.

I sat at the dining room table, phone in hand and dialed the numbers that were written on the paper in front of me. I felt my hands sweat a little. I was nervous! The person on the other end picked up and before long I was being told my future by a young man named Michael. He was very sweet and had a kind voice. He asked me what I wanted to know.

I said, "I would like to know if I will be in a relationship in the future."

"You are going to have a healing." he replied right away. This stumped me!

"My ex-husband?" I asked. I could think of no one I needed a healing with. I had no other people with ill feelings towards me or enemies that I knew of. I was thinking totally different than what he was telling me.

He firmly said, "No, it's not him!"

"I see four men coming into your future actually" he said, and went on to describe each one as I quickly jotted down what he was saying. I still have the paper I wrote on.

"FOUR?" I asked, shocked at the thought. "I only want one," I told him and we laughed. I was a little excited to hear this, whether it would happen or not. There was at least hope.

The first one he started to describe as a young man, 6'2, light brown hair, slender build, good guy who was doing a lot of soul searching and travelling at the time. Jason popped in my mind for a split second and I pushed it back out right away! I wasn't letting my brain go there at all. That was only something I dreamed of.

"Young man? That don't make sense to me at all, I am certainly not into young men." I said.

"I see a young man's face" he continued. I just shrugged it off. Now I doubted this man on the other end of the phone. Even though I believed in psychics, I also believed there are many fakes.

Michael went on to describe the other three men and then said, "There would be relations going on Valentine's Day." I thought, "Right on, it's about time." I had not been with anyone for over two and half years up to that point and was hoping for some much needed romance in my life. The young man was definitely out and it confused me. The descriptions he gave describing three of the men, eventually did come into my life later on. I am still blown away whenever I come across my notes I had taken back then. One of the men Michael described, I had a romantic relationship three years after the reading which lasted for five years and he is still a friend, almost fifteen years later. The other one I met the following September after the reading, fell in love with him but never had any kind of serious relationship with him other than we are also still friends sixteen years later. The descriptions of both these men were distinct and ended up being accurate. The young man he had spoken of baffled me so I had quickly dismissed it. I thanked Michael when the fifteen minutes were up and hung up the phone.

I went to bed around 1 a.m. that night, which was now the New Year, 2000. I was feeling a little bit optimistic for the new millennium and a little sad, I was spending another New Year's Eve alone, especially this special one. What I didn't know, was it was more special than I could ever imagine. My mind went to imagining all the people that were hugging and kissing to bring in the New Year while singing Auld Lang Syne. I longed for that. I wanted a partner and to be part of that group so badly. I would quickly bring myself out of the self-pity mode because I had started to learn by then; this was where my deepest loneliness would stem from, "my thoughts."

After finally falling to sleep, somewhere around 3 a.m. I suddenly awoke and sat straight up in my bed! Goose bumps covered my whole body as the words "my son" and "healing" flashed into my mind. My hands flew up to cover my face and I started to sob. "IT CAN'T BE!" I told myself. "I AM GOING TO MEET MY SON!!!!" I wanted to shout it to the world but it was too late at night to even call my sisters. I would have to stay calm and call them in the morning. I don't think I slept a wink all night before I called all my sisters. Mona was the most closed minded about it all and she didn't get excited or say much, but I didn't care. Donna and my closest friends were cautiously happy for me. I know it was hard for anyone to believe, but I was convinced!

After Christmas, I had already asked for the week of Valentine's Day off at work. My first day off would be Valentine's Day. It would be my first holiday I had booked off since I had started work the year before. This was before the reading ever happened. I didn't book Valentines off for anything special and don't know why I did at the time. "Everything happens for a reason."

My two older children Jesse and Jeanna already knew about Jason, I had told them both when they were old enough to understand, against my ex-husband's wishes. Now I had to tell my youngest daughter Hanna who was nine at the time. I knew after I told her about Jason that I was going to have to tell all three of them that they may meet their brother. I just couldn't tell them how I knew this. I was taking a huge risk but I went with my instinct which is never wrong. I don't always trust in it enough but this time I did. I had my talk with Hanna and she took it very well and was excited to possibly have another brother. My three children never made me feel judged in any way, not once. I am so grateful for that! It says a lot about their character.

I did sit all my kids down and talk to them about the possibility of meeting their brother. I never promised, although I was convinced myself and I never told them how I knew this. I just said, "I have a feeling it might happen." My daughters bought a big, black teddy bear with a plaid scarf wrapped around his neck, to give their brother as a gift when they met him. They seemed to believe too. Even though I tried my best not to get their hopes up too high, my enthusiasm was hard to hide. There was no doubt in my mind it was going to happen! I told all my friends at work. Most were cautiously excited for me, but there was one lady that kept shaking her head. "Not a chance!" she said. I just smiled at that, I knew in my heart that this was going to happen.

Not having any clue when any of this was going to come about, the weeks couldn't go by fast enough for me. I have learned to "live in the moment," much better since then. Remember, the psychic had mentioned, "relations on Valentine's Day" and I already had it booked off before the reading. I was still hopeful I would have a romantic date for Valentine's Day, thinking that was what Michael meant. I had no idea the "relations" he talked about was my actual relatives.

It was the eve before Valentine's Day and my neighbor came to visit me. We always had wonderful chats and he was the one that had given me the number to call the physic. It was my first day off for my holidays the next day and I was a little bummed about not meeting a sweetheart to share Valentine's Day with and for the first time that night I was having a little doubt creep in about the reading. This was nearly six weeks since the reading and I had not heard from anyone or met anyone. My neighbor was trying to keep my spirits up and telling me not to give up. I went to bed that night feeling a little discouraged. The kids were staying with their father that night and I was glad I could at least sleep in and relax on my first day off.

Valentine's Day I woke up at 10 a.m. to my phone ringing. I answered in my sleepy voice and a young lady on the other end said, "Hello, is this Diane Waterman?"

I replied, "Yes it is."

"This is Mary calling from the adoption agency in St. John's Newfoundland," she said.

I nearly fell out of bed!!! I lost it and started crying right away! I was so excited and started telling her how I already knew this was going to happen and about the reading, between my tears of joy! She said I was making her cry too. I didn't know until later that she was actually Jason's adoptive cousin who worked there and made the call to me. That was special!

Mary went on to tell me how Jason had been looking for me too and how we had connected because we had both applied to the agency and registered to try and find each other. She said he was travelling at the time and she would contact me after she talked to him. Nearly twenty five years of wondering and suffering was about to change! I was feeling everything all at once. So many different emotions, fear, excitement, yearning, but mostly love and happiness! It was a glorious day!! I still worried a little that he might hate me, but I felt once he got to know me and we talked, he wouldn't. I hung up the phone, buried my head in my pillow and sobbed from the great relief. This was incredible!!

Now, I was excited to make all the phone calls. This was "the relations on Valentine's Day," that Michael told me about. It was happening, just as he said. It was not how I had thought it would be but this one was a million times better. The relations were about my son and my family. To make it even more special was the fact that it all happened on Valentine's Day.

Needless to say, everyone was in shock! I was excited and emotional! I felt it and believed it, there was no one that could convince me otherwise. This was "our healing," me and my son. The healing Michael had said I was going to have was going to happen. I was on the biggest high of my life!!

A couple of weeks after the first phone call, I heard from Mary one more time after that and she asked, "Is it okay to give Jason your number so he can call you on the following Sunday?" I said, "Definitely!" I was also happy and surprised he still had the same name I had given him, Jason David. I understand his adoptive parents tried to change it but couldn't. The following Sunday morning my phone rang. My girls were as excited as I was. They came running in my room and jumped on my bed as I answered. I said "Hello?" held my breath and waited. A quiet, gentle voice spoke on the other end. "Hello, is this Diane?" I replied, "Yes it is." with the biggest smile on my face!

"This is Jason." He said.

I felt like it was all a dream! I could tell he was a little nervous, as I was, but it was a great first conversation. I was surprised to find out he had been living in Calgary for the past couple of years, just a two and a half hour drive from me but he had been raised in Newfoundland. My kids were thrilled to meet their brother. I was beyond thrilled! I don't think I slept a wink for the next week. He was certainly too old to be held now but I could certainly hug him tight, if he would let me?!

One week later, Jason came to meet his birth family for the first time. Besides giving birth to my other three children, this was probably one of the best things I will ever experience in my life! I was shocked that he looked so much like me when I first saw him. I had always pictured him looking like his birth father. I was crying out with excitement I was so happy!! I hung onto him for dear life. The caretaker came out of her apartment from down the hall to ask me to quiet down. I said, "This is my son, this is my son!!!" I was too excited to let her spoil the moment for us. Jason fit the description that the psychic gave perfectly. He was tall, 6'2, slender and light brown hair. It was a wonderful experience and connection to finally hug him. "A dream come true," for me. It was very healing for both of us, without a doubt! I felt like I had known him forever!

I was 40 years old when I picked up a guitar and first taught myself to play. Jason had started playing guitar around that same time before we met. "I always wondered where my interest in music came from" he said to me. He does very impressive artistic, masonry work. He loves to do paintings and he writes his own songs and poems. He can sing and only sings his own music. We accepted him for the loving soul he is and he accepted us, and for that I am beyond grateful.

Jason speaks highly of his adoptive father and loves him. Jason's birth father had passed away in his mid-forties from throat cancer, but Jason did get to meet his extended family. It was very healing for them as well, especially Jason's grandmother. She was overjoyed! I am happy she got to meet him before she passed away.

It was amazing to meet him and nothing but a great reunion. I had a lot of fears but they were all put to rest quickly. Not all reunions go this way so I was very grateful. Jason never made me feel bad in any way, and I felt he had every right to. He is one of the least judgmental people I have known. His heart is kind and good. I thought about him constantly and had carried more grief from giving him up than I ever knew was possible. I felt for nearly twenty five years, even though I never saw or held him, I always loved him in my heart. I have always felt gratitude and great respect for his adoptive family. I can't give them enough praise and credit, especially his mom.

Jason came to stay with us for the second time a month later. We were all getting along well and the kids and I were enjoying getting to know him better every day. After a few weeks he was getting ready to leave and go back to Calgary. We had said our goodbyes in the morning before I left for work and the kids went to school. When I returned home that evening, I saw a white sheet of paper left on my kitchen table with a poem Jason had written and left for me. The tears flowed as I read his words to me. I saved it in a storage box along with a few other meaningful things from the year 2000.

> *As I travel across this small world,*
> *Tears within my eyes travel across your face.*
> *But with a smile you should know, in this small world you see,*
> *I may be here, I may be there, but I will never be too far away.*
> *Smile, I will see you again soon. Ja xoxo*

My neighbor knocked on my door that evening and told me, Jason had knocked on his door before he left and asked him to keep an eye on me and to make sure I was okay. That really touched my heart. We visited numerous times after that initial visit and I wish I could see him more but I am grateful for any amount of time I have had with him. We talk on the phone on a regular basis, sometimes for hours and he never fails to call me every Valentine's Day for the past sixteen years. I am more than grateful that we had the opportunity to connect and heal. I know it doesn't always go that way for everyone, we are blessed!

Things are very different nowadays with open adoptions. I only wish I had that option when I was eighteen or even had someone to say if you want to keep him, this is how you can do it. I felt completely lost and alone and I felt I had no options. Try to be compassionate towards the mothers who feel they have to give up their baby. It is nearly always done out of love and responsibility to give the child a better life. It is not done out of selfishness, but usually selflessness. I admire and respect the adoptive parents. They are angels in my eyes and deserve to be treated that way.

Today birth mothers very often get to meet and to know the adoptive parents. They get to hold the child, often get to have photos and stay in the child's life for visits. It is set up much better for all involved, especially the child. I understand that not all cases are the same and sometimes complete separation forever is necessary for the sake of the child. Protecting the child should always be number one when it comes to adoptions, especially when a child comes from a situation of abuse or major addictions. Birth mothers were often criticized and judged without even knowing her or anything about her situation. There was a lot of shame put on the birth mother back in 1975 and I am sure there still is to a certain degree today. Believe me, a mother's own guilt is enough. Someone asked me soon after the adoption, "How could you give up your own child?" More shame! These kinds of comments made me shut down even more. I felt like the worse person on the planet, although in my heart I knew I did it from love, putting Jason's needs and future first. The more time that passed without talking to anyone, the more I buried. I grieved for him silently and daily for nearly 25 years.

Hopefully, one day the negative feelings towards birth mothers will be a thing of the past as we are all hopefully being enlightened more and more, to be less judgmental of others. Meeting Jason has been a real blessing for me in my life, whether some believe I deserved it or not. I don't take it lightly. What a privilege it has been!

All I can do now is pass on to others what I have learned from my own experience. Anyone going through this kind of decision, my advice would be to talk about what you're going through with a therapist or counselor that is more readily available nowadays. Openly talk to family, friends and anyone you trust as much as possible about what you are feeling. I hope telling my story will help someone else ease their own pain and help them to stop carrying the "shame" that so many of us birth mothers carry. Forgive yourself, we are human, we do have hearts and we all do the best we can, at the time.

Me and Jason. March 2000

Chapter Ten

Premonitions

Intuition and premonitions are knowing about the future. I have experienced both. Donna experienced them as well as Maye. The earliest ones for me that I can remember were as far back as my early twenties. I didn't know what was going on back then. All I knew was I would sometimes have a glimpse of things that were going to happen, sometimes within seconds or minutes before hand. It was usually a feeling or thought. Sometimes it will come to me in my dreams. Most times at the beginning I was simply confused and thought of it as coincidence. It took years for me to accept it was not. I have a strong intuition. I can feel what others are feeling, sometimes from miles away. I now believe there is no such thing as a coincidence. How we evolve with age!

Sometimes somebody I knew or knew of them would come into my mind and there would be a brief glimpse of something happening to that person. The next day I would hear news that something happened to them. I would talk to my sisters about it and Donna told me many years ago, "the next time it happens pray about it," and so I started doing just that on the rare occasion I was aware of what was happening. It doesn't scare me now because I know it is spiritual and for me is usually connected with people I love. I am simply super sensitive to energy and I pick up on it more than normal. We are all connected as energy, so it makes more sense to me now. It helped me a lot to talk to Donna about it. She shared some of her experiences with me over the years. Some she kept to herself for a long time because she didn't understand it either and it scared her as well. Donna had experienced feelings and signs before a few catastrophes happened in the world. She kept that a secret for a long time before she told me about it. She cried when she finally revealed it to me. She feared she had somehow caused these things to happen. I reassured her at the time that we were only getting a glimpse of what was already in the works. We didn't know what it all meant, much less having control over it and we helped each other as much as we could. We both knew we would get the answers one day.

Sometimes when I have asked my sisters that have passed or God a question to help me when I struggle, I get an answer come to me in a split second without thinking about it. When the answers come quickly without thought, they are usually right on. As I became older I began to accept and believe in it more and more.

Sometimes the premonitions are about someone related to the person I love or am connected to. When I was twenty five, a friend's brother suddenly came into my thoughts, that he was hurt. This brother I had not seen since he was a little boy and now he was an adult. I didn't know him and had no reason to think of him. I remember thinking at the time when he suddenly popped into my head that it was weird for me to think of this young man that I hardly knew. I went on about my day and forgot about it. The next day Mona called me and asked if I had heard about Sheila's brother. She went on to tell me that he had been hurt in a motor cycle accident. I remember telling her that I had a thought about him the day before that he got hurt and I was confused to why I would even think of him. Mona never had these experiences so it was harder for her to understand. I found it hard to believe in the beginning, much less anyone who never experienced it. I shrugged it off and put it out of my mind because it was unexplainable to me. It was easier to think of it as a coincidence. My brother is very intuitive as well although I don't believe he has experienced premonitions.

It would take me many more years to figure out that this was not to be feared but seen as a gift. I had heard of other people experiencing premonitions but I never saw myself in that same light at the beginning. I don't know why, maybe my own fear?!

I was on a road trip back to Fort McMurray from Edmonton with my ex and children back in the early 90's. I remember it was very dark and it was raining hard. Suddenly I became filled with fear to the point of feelings my whole body tighten up. I said to my ex, "Slow down, there is something up ahead," although I could not see anything. He thankfully listened and had just slowed down when we hit a huge pond of water that had gathered on the road and our minivan started to swerve from one side to the other. The kids woke up who were sleeping in the back and my son yelled at his father out of pure fear. My ex thankfully got control of the vehicle but it scared the heck out of all of us. I could only imagine what would have happened if he didn't slow down. I had no idea what was in front of us but I had certainly felt it was dangerous. This is the kind of fear I was talking about earlier. The kind we pay attention to when our intuition speaks to us.

I had many different experiences over the years, like my dad's song playing in my head constantly for two weeks before he died after choosing the photo of him and my mother to frame. I would call that a premonition. I have no control over this, but I do have control over how I handle it. Most times now if I pick up on something, once I get past the initial surprise of it, I find it amazing!

I have learned that highly intuitive and sensitive people are more likely to have these experiences. I can't explain it too much because I am not an expert, but it does make more sense to me now that I have learned from others who talk and write about the universe and its energy and how we are all connected. It also explained to me why I can read people so well. Convincing friends and family who are not believers is another story. It is not that important to me anymore, whether anyone believes me or not. This confidence has come with age and wisdom.

I have often felt grief for no apparent reason only to find out why later. Sometimes it is not my own grief I feel, it is the grief of someone close to me that I am connected to, sometimes before the person I love even knows it is coming. I get premonitions in my dreams, as do my children. When my son Jesse was struggling I dreamt about him every time he was in distress but I didn't know he was, until the next day when I talked to him or a family member. That is the only time I have had dreams about him is when he was near death. Needless to say I never want to dream of him.

I was quite happy to find out recently that my Aunt on my father's side of the family has the same gift that started when she was in her early twenties as well. I had mentioned it to her on the phone and she opened up to me about her own experiences in the past. It was fascinating to me! Now I had an answer to my question of whether this was passed on from past generations in my family. I am pretty sure if I talked to many of my extended family members that live back east and abroad, I would hear a lot of interesting stories. Both my mother and father experienced seeing a ghost when they were young adults, although my father always said he was a non-believer. This never made any sense to me, how someone could see something happen right in front of them and still deny it?! I know now this denial comes from fear. Most people from the past generations would never talk about these experiences at all because it was seen as crazy. This generation is thankfully much more accepting, open minded and aware.

I woke up one morning in October 1992, feeling that something was not right. I was living in Fort McMurray then. I had an overwhelming urge in my chest like I wanted to scream out loud. I couldn't shake it. I never felt this intensity in my chest before in my life for what seemed like no reason. This was another new experience for me and I had no idea why I felt this way.

I got out of bed and got dressed. I went downstairs in my apartment building to check the mail. I decided to go to Junior's place just down the hall from me to try and shake this feeling. He wasn't home but his girlfriend at the time was. I said to Rhonda, "I don't know what's wrong with me today. Ever since I woke up I feel like I want to scream. It's not anything I ever felt before. I had sad days but this is different."

"Oh, you're just having a bad day." she replied.

"No, it's not that," I told her. "I have never felt like this in my life. I feel like someone is going to die." I had never said that before either.

"It is nothing," she said. "It will pass whatever it is," trying to calm me.

I left and was walking back towards my apartment. I could hear my phone ringing as I got closer. I felt sick to my stomach as I walked in and went to the kitchen to answer the phone. I hesitated picking it up. It was my father's voice on the other end. He said "hello," I didn't speak and held my breath. He said, "Diane?"

I whispered, "yes?"

"Your Mom has been taken to the hospital by ambulance. I'm not sure what the problem is, she seemed to have some kind of migraine," he said. Dad sounded serious but stayed calm, for my sake no doubt.

I don't remember what was said after that but I remember how I felt. I was grief stricken and trying not to panic. I heard that soft voice inside my head say, "She's going to die." That scared me! I felt deep down, it was more than a migraine.

I called all my siblings and we all gathered at my place right away. We were on the phone constantly for the next few days. My Mom had a brain aneurism and we were told there was nothing we could do because she was in a coma. We would be called if there was a change or if we needed to go home. All five of us were living in Fort McMurray at the time and my parents were still living in Gander. The doctors did end up doing surgery on my mother and she did survive that one, but she would not survive the second one two months later. Surgery gave her time to spend Christmas with all of us. I am grateful we had that special time with her and got to spoil her one more time. Moms are the glue that holds families together and our family would never be the same again after our mother passed away. How could I know and feel what was going on living so far away from my mother?! I feel the way the universe connects us all is pretty incredible and I do believe God is the source behind it all.

Chapter Eleven
My Baby Sister

It was important for me to write about my relationship with each of my three sisters and how losing each one of them has affected me. I lost my baby sister Maye many years ago, but not in the same way as losing my other two sisters. My youngest sister is my only sister living now and she resides in Ontario. Our family lost her to addiction and sadly her own "shame" a long time ago.

Unfortunately, Maye's spirit was broken when she was a very young child. By the time she was twelve she was experimenting with drugs and alcohol. Maye's addictions became worse over the years and peaked after our Mom died in 1992. The following year was when Maye left Fort McMurray and the last time I saw her.

Maye is nearly four years younger than me. She was our pretty, little baby doll. There were numerous early signs of issues with our little sister. It started when she was seven years old and she started skipping school. Mom would send one of us to look for Maye when she didn't come home. She set Christmas paper on fire in our home around that time as well, that our father quickly put out. Things got worse as she got older. It would be many decades later before we figured why she did these things. I do feel regret for not spending more time with her as growing children. I don't believe it would have changed anything that happened to her but maybe she would not have felt alone, as I believe she did as a child. Our age differences left her more vulnerable. Mona,

MY BABY SISTER

Donna and I were close in age and had many of the same friends. As Maye got older and started using alcohol and drugs, it seemed she did not want us in her circle of friends. I felt brushed off many times when it came to her friends. That is the way it is in families when dealing with addiction. It was hard not to take it personally but when it comes to major addictions, friends who use will always come first. We may not have had any control over what went on as kids but we could have helped her more as adults if she would have been able to open up to us. Her shame kept her quiet.

When we were teenagers, my sister was using drugs and alcohol on a regular basis. She would disappear for days at a time. These were the times when we had our biggest arguments. I remember worrying about how this was affecting our mother, not having a clue why my sister was acting this way. Even though Mom didn't say much to Maye, I knew she had to be worried. Maye would have been around fifteen at this time. She had her own set of friends and we never knew where she was. My sisters and I would hear things from friends that worried me.

Maye was always a big concern in our family. Any time I tried talking to her and asking what was going on it became an argument. I am sure I approached it all wrong. What did I know as a teenager about addiction? Nothing, other than I loved her and worried about her. The older we got the more I became concerned about her, as did my other siblings. It had to be torture for our parents.

Maye left home by the time she was twenty, married her childhood sweetheart and they had three children. Her husband was in the Navy and she was left alone a lot with three small children. She got involved in substance abuse again and again, which eventually led to all of her children being taken from her, including the three she had later on in her life. It was a tragedy beyond belief for everyone involved! Mom told me later that Maye called her on the phone, screaming like a child, devastated by what she had done. I do know she was a good and loving mother when she was sober. I believe Maye has led a tortuous life.

My family and I had tried everything we could to protect her and her children when she lived with us in Fort McMurray. We kept a close eye on them and many times left our own families night after night when we knew Maye was using, to watch over her children. Why our baby sister would do the things she did was mostly confusing for me and my family. A puzzle we couldn't figure out.

I found out many years later Maye was sexually abused by a much older, extended family member as a child and from what I know now; it went on for many years. This is not an excuse for her but I do believe it definitely changed who she might have become. She had no support at all in all those years and by the time we found out she was almost 30 years old.

The abuse would have started happening to her when she was about seven, which is around the time she started acting out and skipping school in grade two. Finding this out was heartbreaking but I am glad I did because it answered many questions for me and my family and now Maye would finally have some support. The problem was, she still couldn't open up to us. Her pain and shame runs deep!

We could finally fit a big piece of the puzzle together. Suddenly everything made sense to me. All the years that I would hear people ask, "Why is Maye so different from the rest of you?" as in, her addictive behavior and getting into trouble? Now I knew. I was heartbroken for her and I was angry it happened to her. I often wonder what her life would be like and how productive she would have become if this never happened to her. I believe her whole life would have been so different. I do believe it's never too late to heal with determination and will. My sister has been through so much in her 55 years and there's a lot I pray she can forgive herself and others for. I don't give up on anyone I love until one of us is no longer breathing. Sometimes all it takes is for one person to believe in you and I am that one person.

Nobody ever talked about anything sexual back then or warned us about the possibilities that this could even happen. It was taboo in our family in the sixties and seventies. We trusted family. If someone was brave enough to tell a parent back then, many times they were not believed or told to keep it quiet. It was brushed under the rug a lot. She needed someone to protect her and I feel she was let down, mostly because of the lack of awareness back then. Everything was tight lipped back then as well and the worse scenario for me to find out would be that someone did know and turned their back on her. What hurts even more is remembering some of the beatings she got as a young girl because she was "acting out" like many abused children naturally do. It was cruel! I can't even imagine how she felt. 'Lost and alone' comes to mind. She wouldn't have known herself why she was acting out.

The "shame" she carried all those years she tried to bury with alcohol and drugs. She has never talked to any of our immediate family about what happened to her but she made comments to other trusted family members that confirmed it had happened to her. I wish she could have been more open and found the strength to tell us, her sisters. I would never have judged her. Her sisters would have tried to protect her and help her, without a doubt! I would imagine she was manipulated into keeping it quiet for years. Maye was not the only one affected by this family member, there were others but Maye's life was affected by it the most. Maybe because it happened more frequent and went on longer than the others did. She was also given beer as a child and nobody knows the whole truth about the extent of the abuse. Everybody is different and we all have different strengths in how we handle life in general. My sisters and I could never blame her because she was never at fault for anything that happened to her as a child or young girl, period!

"Shame" instilled by adult acts, never ceases to amaze me. It angers me to the core that little kids and young people abused by adults, ever have to carry any shame. How the abused child acts out as they get older is a complete side effect from what has been done to them. The "acting out" and addictions of many, only adds to even more shame and the cycle continues. Everybody this happens to handles it differently but there is much in common. Bad things happen to many good people and that will never change. What can change is, WE as a society could let go of that one thing that causes so much destruction in our homes, families and our souls and that is "shame." I believe it would change the world if we could all be completely open and never worry about being judged. It would also stop a lot of abuse. We are doing better than thirty or forty years ago for sure, but we have a lot more work to do. We can and should give support for anyone willing to fight and be well. Openness, awareness, therapy and treatments have greatly improved. So has parenting because of the awareness and openness.

The choices that each of us decide as adults, we ultimately have to live with. Although my sister fought many times to stay clean, it is a battle she can't seem to win for long. I do have hope that Maye will have a healthier life, one that she deserves. She did tell me in our last phone call, she doesn't drink anymore but she is still using drugs. I admired the honesty. I had not heard from her for over two years since just before Mona passed away. She had been in rehabilitation again but left early. I was pleased when she finally did call me. I do worry about her still. Many times over the years Maye gave our family phone numbers that most times we could never get hold of her on. She told me the reason I don't hear from her more is because of the shame and guilt she carries. I said "It's time to let that go. We are not young anymore and life is short. No more shame Maye, let it go!"

I know the things Maye has done in her life that she carries the most shame about is not who she is at the core. I remember her before the abuse and addictions. Her innocence was stolen from her and it changed her but I know deep down, she is a very sweet and kind person. What she has done to survive and keep her addictions alive, is a reaction to what was done to her. I know it ripped her apart when her children were taken and the shame from that alone would be more than anyone could ever imagine. These are not excuses for her; this is a reality that goes on in our world every day. I hate that none of us could help her. I hope this might in some small way.

I told Maye I was writing about her in my book. She said "Oh Lord." There was a nervous chuckle. I had no plans on being hard on her, she's been through enough. She has an open mind and I believe with being in rehabilitation so many times, she has hopefully healed some things. If talking about this helps one more person, I believe that would make her very happy. I don't want anyone who is related to the family member who abused my sister to feel any shame either. We have no control over anyone else's actions and this kind of thing unfortunately happens in many good families.

Maye loves to sing, read and write as well. She loves writing poetry and she loves art. She kept a very clean home and took good care of her children in the good years. She is very creative and she is also very sensitive to the spiritual world. Maye has a history of being with some really mean men as well, not surprisingly. I know she has lived a very hard life, and I might not know her as well as I would like after twenty four years, but I miss her. I do stay in contact with some of her children and they are beautiful adults raised by good families. I am fortunate and grateful that they let me be a part of their lives, even in any small way. Only one daughter has any contact with Maye. I understand they all have their own feelings about Maye, and I respect that as I know she does.

I just recently told Maye I was sorry for all she went through in her life. The thought came to me just after I talked to her in that last phone call and I felt an urgency to say it to her, so I sent her a text right away. I don't know why I have never said that to her before, maybe because I never understood her or had enough contact with her or wisdom before now. She stayed in contact more with Mona because Mona and her husband adopted one of Maye's daughter's. Either way, it needed to be said by someone in her family. She replied to me in a text, "I just drew a good, long breath. Long time coming. Thank you Sis, I love you." I talked to her one other time a few weeks later and it was a more emotional call. I could tell she was hurting. At one point before we hung up she started to cry and said, "I just want to be five years old again with all my sisters around me." I understood her pain because there are times I feel the same way, missing that sisterly bond. It broke my heart! I love you too baby sister, you are not alone! Be safe!!

Maye. 1971

Chapter Twelve
Cancer Hits Home

I don't remember a lot about what lead up to my sister Donna going to see a doctor back in 1973, other than she had some swelling in her neck. The way things were back then in most families was everything was kept quiet from the children. I had no idea what was going on until weeks after the first doctor appointment, after my parents and sister came back from a trip to St. John's. We were living in the little community of Clarke's Head, NL back then.

I was standing at the kitchen sink when my mother told us that my sister had "Hodgkin's Disease," a form of cancer that had attacked her lymph nodes. I remember very clearly, the fear I felt right away. I was speechless as I looked at my sister sitting there with her head hung down. It was in late summer and I left the house and ran out into the garden. I went in the back yard where the clothes line and raspberry and strawberry bushes were, and I hid away behind a bush where no one could find me and I wept. I was shocked that this was happening to my sister who was also my best friend. Everything was running through my head, but most of all, is she going to die? My sister was only fifteen years old and I was sixteen.

I went back inside after what seemed like hours. Donna was upstairs in her bedroom. I went to her and we just sat on the bed and hugged each other and cried, without speaking a word. We didn't have to say anything, we understood each other. I knew she was scared and I was scared for her. We were so connected sometimes we would start singing the same line from a song at the same time. We would laugh out loud whenever that happened, it always surprised us and now I didn't know if my soul mate would survive cancer. I was angry for a while wondering, "Why her?" She was so quiet, sweet and innocent.

I don't remember how many months she went away to St. John's for radiation treatments, but Donna was gone often over the next several months. Mom let me go with them one time. I remember being at the hospital, standing at my sister's bedside before she went for her treatment. She had burn marks around her neck area that turned from red to brown over time, from the radiation. I don't ever remember her complaining, she was so quiet about it all.

Donna lost all of her hair which had to be devastating to a fifteen year old. I don't remember her saying anything or getting upset about it. I am certain she was heartbroken when she was alone, but she kept it to herself. Her heart was very tender and I knew enough to hug her often. There was a scar on her neck where they had done the biopsy. I worried about if she would die the whole time.

Back then, death was the end result a lot of the time whenever we heard of someone with cancer. The fear was very real to me and like I said, nobody filled us in on what the doctors were saying along the way. I am sure our parents didn't know everything either and anything they shared with the adults in their families was kept from us. I can't imagine what they went through at the time.

The winter came and went and my sister started to look better. Finally after the treatments were over, we were told the cancer was gone! She would have to go for checkups for a while. This was very exciting news and I remember being very happy and relieved! Her hair started to grow back thick and very curly.

Donna graduated high school and then she moved back to Goose Bay where Mona had already moved with her husband. They had their first child together, a son, who my family adored and doted on. It wasn't too long before I moved back there as well. Things were looking up for my sister Donna, and no one was more thrilled than I was. We were all happy to be living together again and that Donna was doing so well.

Chapter Thirteen
Second Time

Donna's second battle with cancer occurred at the age of twenty five in 1983. Ten years after the first time! This time, we were all living in Fort McMurray. My sisters and I had moved there in 1978 with our own families we were raising by then. Donna had become very ill, and started losing weight. It took the medical doctors a full year to find out that the cancer had returned. By the time they finally diagnosed her, her skin had turned very yellow and she had lost 80 pounds. She made several trips to Edmonton seeing specialists before they finally found the cancer. Why it took so long to find it is beyond me. Saving money on the expensive testing I am certain.

    I do remember her saying after one trip to Edmonton, that she had overheard one of the doctors say "I can feel something," while checking her spleen and stomach area with his hands. Still, they did no more testing while she was there and sent her home again saying there was nothing. Surely after having cancer once before, you would think they would have done the necessary tests. We all could visually see that she had swelling in her back area.

    I have learned years later, after going through some of the testing routines with Mona and how it works, the testing starts at the cheapest cost. I know there are rules to go by to control health care costs and I understand not all similar symptoms people have result in cancer but when all the signs are there and especially if there is cancer in someone's past, do the tests!

The "pet scan," they used on my sister Mona's lungs, showed the cancer right away after her suffering and trying other tests for months. By the time they found the cancer in Donna the second time around, it had already spread to most of her organs including her liver. The PET scan should have been used at the first signs with Donna, not almost a year later when she looked near death. This made me very angry! My family was told that, she had a 50/50 chance of survival. It was very upsetting that she had to get so sick before it was finally discovered.

The doctors gave Donna two options, six months of chemotherapy or surgery. She chose the chemo and I was grateful she did, because I believed, if she chose the surgery she may not have survived it.

Donna started the treatments and she suffered terribly with every chemo treatment. She was throwing up a lot after each treatment. I would kneel behind her sometimes and wrap my arms around her slim, bony waist, holding her snug while she leaned over the toilet to throw up so it wouldn't hurt her so much. It was very heartbreaking and I felt helpless that I couldn't make it better for her. Being strong and supportive is all you can do at those times when a loved one is suffering.

After about two months into this, I went to visit Donna one day in particular and she was still in bed. When I had called earlier in the day to check on her, Mona had told me she couldn't get her to get out of bed. Every day I went to see her and she had never stayed in bed all day, I was worried. When I arrived, I went downstairs where she was lying in her bed and I sat next to her. One thing I knew for sure as we got older and Donna had become more talkative, is that she would open up to me.

She lay limp in the bed and I asked her "what's wrong Sis?" I could see depression written all over her face and in her body language. She was lifeless. All her strength had been drained from her body and she had given up. It was not surprising with her being so sick but I wasn't about to give up on her. She whispered to me "I just want to die, I'm tired of it all." We both wept quietly and I gently rubbed her back. My heart broke in two. I understood how she felt as much as I could without being in her shoes. I was scared! I clearly remember how I spoke to her next. "C'mon, let's get you up." I stated, as I stood up next to the bed. Not asking her if she wanted to get up so she had a choice. I knew she would decline if I asked. Donna didn't argue with me as I gently pulled the covers off her frail body. Her body was the smallest I had ever seen her. She was tall at 5'9, so I expect she was probably down to 120 pounds by then. I got her out of bed, helped her upstairs to the main level and sat her at the table. She ate very light but loved to eat dried fruit. Apricots were her favorite, anything with lots of flavor because she couldn't taste a lot at the time.

The doctors were giving her a strong pain killer with codeine in it for the pain. Little did any of us know back then how addictive these pills were and how it would affect my sister in the future. None of us were aware of the side effects of any drugs back then. I spent the day there with her and made sure she was okay before I left to go home. I talked to Mona and filled her in so she was aware of what happened and could keep an eye on her. That was one of Donna's darkest moments at that time that I am aware of.

Donna was staying with Mona at the time. Mona and her family were living in a house that had a finished basement. Donna and her family lived in a mobile home as did my family and it was decided for Donna to stay at Mona's until she felt better. Mona seemed to thrive on taking care of everything and everyone, so no one argued with her. I used to resent Mona sometimes for being that way. My other sisters felt the same way sometimes. The rest of us had no say in anything we might have wanted to do. Anything we suggested always seemed to be frowned upon or ignored. Now when I look back, I believe being the oldest in the family, Mona might have always felt responsible for everyone. Not easy for her I am sure, feeling that kind of pressure. She seemed to thrive on it though. We would argue sometimes about her not wanting to let someone else take care of things, but it never went over well. We could only do our part and I made sure I was there every day to help as much as I could, even if it was just to keep Donna's spirits up and hold her when she threw up.

Now when I look back I see everything a little differently. When we were young we thought we had it all figured out, I believe now at age 60, I am only beginning to learn about people's behavior and what is really behind their actions. Things are definitely not always how they seem. That has also been one of the biggest lessons I have learned about life.

Donna's treatments went on for five months before the cancer was gone. We were all elated with the good news! To be honest I was very surprised she was cured, considering the cancer had been in her liver. We had been told by a medical professional that once it was in the liver the chances were very slim of survival. I wondered for a long time afterwards if the little glass of Aloe Vera juice that my sister drank every morning while she had her treatments had anything to do with her healing. I have always believed it might have. She had been so ill before the cancer was even found. It was miraculous! If I was a cancer patient today,

I would try the juice along with the other treatments, if it is approved by the Doctor.

It wasn't long after this second battle with cancer that I started to see a change in Donna. She was always funny, quick witted, kind, compassionate, nonjudgmental, open minded, very giving and stubborn as a mule. None of those character traits changed but her moods did. My sister had now become addicted to pain medicine. Her addiction would not only cause many mood swings but eventually caused a chemical imbalance. Between the chemicals from the over usage of pills along with all the chemicals from the chemo treatments, my sister became bipolar in her final years. All the chemicals that she had ingested had affected her brain function over time. For the next twenty five years she would now fight her addiction to pain medication.

It was devastating to all of us to see her suffer like that. Donna became very depressed at times as the years went on. After all she had been through and now this?! It just didn't seem fair for one person to have to go through so much suffering in her life time. Not only did this affect her, but her family as well.

Our parents came from Newfoundland to visit when Donna was sick in 1983. It did her a world of good for them to be there and to have our family all together in one place, for what would be the last time. I have only one photo of all seven of us together, and it's from that time. I usually cringe when I see any photo of myself in my chubbier days but then I look at Donna and see how sick she was and I don't cringe anymore. She always managed to have a smile on her face. This photo has become very precious to me.

Maye, Donna, Diane, Mona, Dad, Junior, and Mom. 1983

Chapter Fourteen
Donna's Many Health Issues

In 2002, at the age of forty five, Donna found out she had Hepatitis C, contracted from a blood transfusion she had received as part of the cancer treatments in 1983. This was a shock to her and us that she had been inflicted with this disease for almost twenty years and didn't know. I thought, "My God, what next?!" She refused the treatments for this disease after talking to her doctor because they would have been way too hard on her. She was told by her doctor, "The treatments are intense." She chose to carefully live with the Hepatitis C, for the rest of her life.

In 2005, Donna had open heart surgery to replace her heart valve with a cow's valve. It was a big surgery. She took it all in stride, never losing her great sense of humor. She always amazed me with her strength and strong will.

Donna had stayed with me before the heart surgery and it was a special time for me, having her here in Edmonton. I loved every minute! I would go to work and come home to having my favorite person in the world to talk to. Our many hours of conversation were always fun, filled with laughter, sometimes emotional and always meaningful to me. I always enjoyed her company.

After the heart surgery, the first couple of hours of recovery were a nightmare for my sister. She woke up in a panic and was not treated well by a nurse and doctor, who were ignoring her cries out for help. She was on a ward with many others from surgery. Nobody let us know she was awake or in this state after she woke up from surgery. She had been asking for her family and she was being ignored until a woman who wasn't her nurse, I believe she may have been from housekeeping or an assistant, was sympathetic enough to get my phone number from Donna and the woman called me. "Your sister needs you to come now!" she said firmly. Mona, Donna's husband and I rushed to the hospital ward. Her husband went in to see her first and then he rushed back out to us to say she was upset and wanted to see me. I rushed to the ward where she was. My sister was lying in her bed distraught and sobbing loudly. I said, "My God, what's wrong?" She kept telling us through her stammering and crying she was being ignored and laughed at. She had been begging the nurse to call me and the nurse wouldn't. Then my sister pointed and said, "Look at them" and I turned and saw that my sister was not being paranoid. I had never seen any patient, much less a heart patient so disrespected in my entire life! I saw with my own eyes my sister's nurse standing a few feet away, whispering to a coworker, watching us and laughing at my sister who was so distraught. I was so angry to see this behavior I wanted to scream at the nurse but I kept my cool! I was shocked by it all and I felt like I must have been in a movie. My sister had been in hospitals so many times over the years and not once had she had a problem with the doctors or nurses. They always loved her and treated her with respect, as she did them. It is still hard for me to accept that patients get treated this way, especially at a hospital that was held with such high regard. I approached the laughing nurse and her co-worker as calmly as I could, and said a few words as calmly as I could. She stopped laughing.

My sister kept sobbing and trying to tell me what happened. It was when I told her "I believed you" that the doctor suddenly came straight to my sister's bed side and asked if there was a problem? I knew he had overheard me. I kept wiping the tears and sweat off her face with a cool cloth and kept trying to calm her down. Donna put him in his place. She was angry and asked him, "Why were you ignoring me every time you walked past my bed when I asked you for help?" I did know the doctor had walked by her bed a couple of times while I was standing next to her and he didn't even look her way or try to help us in any way. I looked at the doctor and asked, "What is going on?" The doctor said he had been busy with other patients. I was dumbfounded to say the least. This was a ward for recovering "open heart surgery patients." How can they ignore someone who is distraught after waking up from having open heart surgery?! There were no curtains drawn. The whole ward was wide open and anyone there could see my sister needed help. I didn't witness one other patient there who seemed to be in trouble. It blew me away and still makes me angry to this day. "Sis, if you don't calm down, I am going to pass out!" I said. And I meant it. I could feel my legs wanting to buckle under me. In those years my own anxiety levels were at their worst. That was when Donna finally took some deep breaths and calmed down. I was really scared she was going to have a major heart attack right in front of me and none of the staff seemed to care, except the lady who called us to come. Donna did point her out to me and I whispered a thank you to her as she passed by us at one point. I didn't want to get her in trouble for calling us. The doctor said very little that I can remember other than they would be moving her to a room and I was happy about that. I did hear after this terrible event that there were many horror stories about this hospital. I wouldn't have believed it if I had not witnessed it with my own eyes.

I have woken up from surgery a couple of times over the years crying and not knowing why. There was always a nurse close by to reassure me I was okay. They were always compassionate. After the last surgery I had eight years ago for my gallbladder, I remember while waking up hearing one nurse ask the other if I was still crying. I had to have been crying while I was still asleep. This is quite normal in many cases the nurse told me afterwards. The way my sister was treated was horrible! I wanted Donna to file a complaint after she got out of there and felt better, but she didn't. I think she was happy to have survived and just wanted to forget it ever happened.

It is painful to remember how Donna was treated, but once she got off the recovery ward and put in a semi-private room, she did very well. She was very happy to be alive and well. The nurses and doctor there treated her great!

Up until the heart surgery, Mona and Donna had not spoken for six months because they had a falling out. Thankfully, just before the surgery, they made up and Mona came to the hospital. Siblings have falling outs sometimes but this was a long time for them not to speak. When Donna was released from the hospital Mona offered to take care of her if need be, once they got back to Fort McMurray. Donna and her husband ended up staying with Mona and her husband for eight months because Donna had many complications. Donna couldn't have asked for a better care taker than Mona and in the end, that time they spent together healed their strained relationship and they became closer than ever.

Donna had many physical needs at that time, and Mona was a great nurse and loved this opportunity to be needed. Mona was learning to be less judgmental and more understanding of our sister. I was happy for them, but a little upset that I was living in Edmonton and couldn't help them more. I felt guilty about it. I did ask Donna to stay with me and I would care for her as much as I could. I was working forty hours a week, so she would have to be alone for those hours. Donna didn't want to stay here in Edmonton which was understandable considering her family was living in Fort McMurray.

Donna had also developed osteoporosis years before and had lost two inches off her height. Her neck became even more bent over from sleeping in a wheelchair as well, for months after her heart surgery. She had some therapy to try and strengthen and straighten her neck, although it helped, it never went back to normal. My sister, who was always the same height as me now had to look up at me when we stood next to each other. As I write this I can picture her sweet face with those blue eyes that would look up at me with her reading glasses perched low on her nose. The memory tugs on my heartstrings.

Donna developed huge water blisters on her legs, some the size of your fist, after the heart surgery. She felt she couldn't breathe properly when she tried lying down, so she would sit up and sleep in the chair. That caused more problems because her legs were not lifted. All the fluids would go to her legs and that didn't help with the blisters. Some of it was caused from the medications and the surgery itself. Eventually, she got better after trying many different things. Mona deserves so much credit for changing those bandages on Donna's legs every day. They had a home nurse help out too and we were grateful for her help. I went to Fort McMurray to see them and I tried changing her bandages. It was not an easy job and I was nervous doing it, afraid I would hurt her.

I don't know of anyone who could have survived the things Donna survived and come out of it with their sanity still intact. The addiction to the pain medication would be a battle for her up until the year before her death. It changed her as a person in many ways, but I still knew who my sister was deep down. She was a compassionate, good soul, who had been dealt a cruel hand in life and she handled it the best she could.

I had many heated arguments with Mona over the years about Donna's antics as she got into her mid to late forties. The arguments between Mona and I were more frequent in the last couple of years of Donna's life. I couldn't listen to the constant negative remarks anymore. I didn't judge Donna. Everyone was entitled to their own opinion about their experience in dealing with her addiction and behavior but I didn't want to be talking badly about her behind her back. I had compassion for her because I knew she did not pick up pain medication one day and decide to become an addict. This addiction was caused from her having to take them when she was very ill and in a lot of pain from the cancer and the treatments. It wasn't a choice, it was necessary. Donna accepted she had a problem and was honest about her addiction. I admired that.

There were some 3 o'clock in the morning phone calls when Donna would be at one of her low points and I always answered. Sometimes when I would answer her calls of desperation, I wouldn't recognize who it was on the other end of the phone because she could hardly talk she would be in so upset. She sounded like a little child on the other end. I was glad that she trusted me enough to call me. She knew I would always help her and have her back. This happened at least forty times over the last 10 years of her life. Sometimes it happened during the day, sometimes at night. I would have to ask sometimes, "Donna, is that you?" She could barely whisper a "yes," sobbing uncontrollably. I would be patient and tell her to take deep breaths and give her time to try and talk to me. She had always been so sensitive already in her true self, and now with this disease, she was a hundred times more sensitive. I hated hearing her on these downward spirals when her feelings were hurt. It was magnified by the disease. I understand she was not always easy to deal with sometimes, but I still had her back. The alternative did not exist for me. Bipolar can cause very high highs and very low lows. These calls were at her lowest.

I would listen to her for at least an hour or two on every phone call. I would give her advice to help her cope, but mostly I just listened and let her vent. There were times that I was very honest to her, in a kind but firm way when she would be upset with others. I would tell her if I thought she was wrong, and she would always listen to my reasoning and not get upset with me. It was done with respect. All my sister ever wanted was support from me, and I gave it to her the best I could. The pills were messing her up big time in her perception of the world around her, but I knew Donna's heart, and all that mattered to me at her low times was to get her through another day. I always made her promise me that she would be okay before I would hang up. I knew she would keep her word to me because I could hear it in her voice. I never hung up, especially to try and go back to sleep, until I felt she was safe. Making her laugh was key and always seemed to do the trick.

Donna was finally diagnosed with bipolar and put on medication for it. She was more like her true self that last year than she had been for many years before. I don't believe she was using the pain medication in that last year of her life. The phone calls of desperation stopped and we would have normal conversations, always making each other laugh about something silly. She always wanted to know details of what was going on in my love life. "What love life?" I would jokingly say. Donna always wished I could find a good man to share my life with. I know she didn't like me living alone. She had told me several times that she admired my courage. I told her there was no one on the planet as courageous as her in my eyes. It was either a good laugh or a good cry by the end of our calls. I miss those phone calls more than anything in the world.

Many times my sister became very irritable coming off the pills. Like any drug that is abused, it causes mood changes. It was very hard on her immediate family and caused a lot of friction. I don't blame any of them for how they felt, most times it was justified I'm sure. I just wanted to protect her. I felt like her twin in many ways during our life time together and I understood her. We certainly had some disagreements over the years, but it never lasted long. We forgave each other easily.

After Donna's heart surgery, when she was feeling better, she became upset about some family members not answering her calls. I told her straight up, "You and your husband caused the rifts in your family with both of you gambling and your addiction to pills." I wanted her to be more understanding of how addiction affected family and friends because I had learned a thing or two by then. I have learned when people are in their addiction and own world, nothing else matters but the next high, no matter what form of drug it is. Compulsive gambling is one of the worse and can definitely cause mood swings and depression as well. The highs and lows are the same as any other addiction. When I was with her, I could see a light bulb come on in her brain and she looked at me with this knowing look. She was thinking, and then she would slowly nod her head to agree with me. I certainly never wanted to be preachy to her, just for her to understand where the other family members who would be upset with her might be coming from. I felt she understood in the end.

As much as I loved her, she had to take responsibility and I knew when I was respectfully straight with her she would be honest about herself. I know her mind was not clear enough when she was using to be able to see her mistakes and where she went wrong. There were other times when she was clean, I knew it became clear to her and she got it. She did have common sense, but when she was high she just couldn't see anything clearly, just her own needs.

We respected each other enough to be honest and I believe she was glad I was up front with her in the end. I saw a big change in her family that last year. She took the responsibility and I was very glad to see some closeness return with her and her children. I know she loved them with all her heart. I know she missed them all and had many regrets by that point in her life. I am happy she finally had some sort of resolution before her death.

There were a couple of times over the years Donna had called me to say she was struggling with the pills and wanted to stop taking them. This woman fought her disease. I remember asking her in one incident if she had any on her now. She told me "yes, I have some in my purse and my housecoat pocket. I have around twenty or thirty pills." I asked her to go flush them down the toilet while I was on the phone with her, and she did. I never doubted her. I noticed a change in her a few days later. I knew she had won the battle for another little while at least. She was clean for almost a year after that call. I always felt her determination and trusted her completely when she gave me her word, high or not. It is not easy for anyone to deal with the highs and lows of any addict who was also now bipolar. We all did our best in our own way.

One thing I know for sure about Donna. She would definitely want me to be completely honest in writing this book. I feel she is guiding me and helping me every step of the way. Sometimes my sister was taking sixty or more pain meds a day when she was using. Ask your doctor for other pain relief choices if possible, than those with codeine in them.

Chapter Fifteen
Losing My Soul Mate

Donna had been through hell again in the last few years of her life with sickness. I worried about her constantly. Cancer had returned to her breasts this time, and she was now on a drug that made her very sick. I noticed the difference in her within weeks after she started taking the drug. She had been cancer free for twenty five years since the last battle. One year after her heart surgery at the age of fifty, they removed her breasts. The doctors could not give her any more treatments of radiation or chemo therapy because of her past treatments with both. They would normally do the other treatments as precautionary and to make sure they got all the cancer. This new drug that was being offered to her would keep her in remission and supposedly keep her alive for two more years. I don't know the name of the drug but if you research "drugs used to keep cancer patients in remission" there are many that are listed. I am sure it may work for some people but like all other drugs, there are side effects. The doctor said Donna could choose not to take it and live her life as long as she could without it. It was a grim prognosis and our hearts were all broken!

    I was at the oncologist with her as was her husband and Mona when she received the devastating news. My heart sank and the tears flowed. The oncologist left us alone for us to discuss it and for Donna to make her decision. I believe we were all in shock at first. My first thought was 'don't take the drug' after we listened to all the side effects, but ultimately it was up to her.

Of course we wanted to have her with us as long as possible, but after watching how much she suffered for much of her life, I personally thought her "quality of life" was most important. I didn't want her to suffer even more. I did try to express that to her. I believed she could survive the two years, maybe longer without it. I would love to see her live and enjoy her $65,000 owed to her from the government for the Hepatitis C she had contracted in 1983. I wanted for her to see her dream fulfilled of going back to Newfoundland for a family holiday. She deserved every penny of that money and more. None of us knew if the cancer would ever come back. After a brief discussion with us, it was her final decision to take the drug.

The drug clearly took a negative effect on her right away and for the remainder of the four months she lived after that. I prayed she would at least get to have her trip back home when she finally received her check two months later, but that never happened.

When I saw her again on a trip to Fort McMurray a few weeks after she started taking the drug, she was visibly depressed, which was one the side effects I worried about. She was nauseated, couldn't eat, and her face was flushed. She looked like she had a fever. I could see this drug had caused hormonal changes in her body. I was very concerned because she had been doing so well mentally in that last year. I talked to her about how she was feeling and all she did was weep. Silent tears rolled down her cheeks when she told me how horrible she was feeling. "I can see the difference in you from a few weeks ago and I hate seeing you like this." I said. I was very upset that she was suffering, yet again. She did continue to take the drug. That's how much my sister loved life!

Donna and I had talked about death several times over the years and as we became older, we both agreed, we did not want death but we did not fear it either. To endure all the sickness she had been through in her lifetime and survive it all was miraculous in itself. I couldn't imagine what those years were like for her. I could understand that feeling of being exhausted and having chronic pain, having experienced fibromyalgia for much of my adult life but it came nowhere close to all she had suffered and survived. I love life and I know she did as well. Donna was a fighter in every way, through all her illnesses.

On December 18, 2008, when I got home from working at a jewelry store at Kingsway Mall, I decided to call Sis. After a few rings went in, Donna answered the phone and her voice sounded weak. Just a minute into the conversation she asked me "Can you come for Christmas?"

"I'm sorry Sis they won't give me time off at work this time of year." I replied. It was just one week before Christmas. I knew it would be impossible to get time off now. "But, I will definitely try and take some time off right after Christmas and come see you." I said. She seemed okay with that. "Is everything okay?" I asked. She said she couldn't eat and was stomach sick all the time. I now believe she may have felt her death was near. Donna was very intuitive.

I felt guilty that I couldn't go. The jewelry business makes it quite clear that you don't take time off at Christmas, unless it is an emergency. I had taken time off twice in the past few months and went to Fort McMurray to see her. My funds were very low as well at the time. I would get a Christmas bonus just after Christmas and it would be easier for me to go then.

Although I felt this phone call was not one of her desperate calls, it still bothered me. I had worried about her constantly since I last saw her. Before we hung up she said, "I am tired of being sick."

I said, "I understand Sis." and I did get it!

I was going to make sure I went to see her right after the Christmas rush. We told each other that we loved each other and that I would see her soon and we hung up. She knew I understood her suffering and would never judge her for giving up the battle she had fought since she was fifteen years old. "She will be okay." I told myself. I thought of calling Mona, but I was exhausted from a busy shift and went to bed. So many times I tell myself I am just being silly and over thinking things, when I should always go with my gut! I prayed she would hang on and hopefully get past this bad time, like she did so many other times before. I just needed to go see her and then everything would be okay.

The last time I saw Donna and Mona was at a Celine Dion concert in October, two months earlier. Mona, Donna, my niece and her friend had all come to Edmonton for the concert. Donna had never been to a concert in Edmonton and we were all excited to go to this one together. Mona had bought the ticket for me for my birthday in September and I was elated! It was the first time in many years that we were going to a concert together. I met up with them all at the hotel across from where I worked and we were on our way.

I sat in the seat between my two sisters and watched probably the best performance any of us would ever witness. It was electrifying! There were certain songs like, "The Power of Love," that Donna and I would just look at each other with tears in our eyes, because it was songs we had loved for so many years and to hear it live was emotional for us. We were deeply moved by the music that night. Mona loved it as much as we did for sure but she didn't get emotional. She was tougher than Donna and I. We wore our hearts on our sleeve.

After the concert we all went back to the hotel. After working all day, I was exhausted. We sat around and we talked about the concert for a while, then I said my goodbyes. Donna's daughter and her friend had already gone back to their room. I hugged Mona and then Donna and went home. If I had only known this was the last time I would ever see Donna alive, I would have hung on a lot longer and tighter.

Two days after my phone call with my sister we had a gift exchange at work. It was December 20th. I was very excited to receive a Celine Dion cd with all her hits on it from my coworker Dan. It was such a thoughtful and perfect gift after seeing her in concert with my sisters. I loved it!! My boss had also given me a special gift. It was a book titled "The Four Agreements." It was about wisdom by the author, "Don Miguel Ruiz." These two gifts would have more significance for me in the near future than I knew. I had asked my boss for time off after Christmas to go see my sister for a few days. She said "we would work something out." I was relieved, happy and excited to tell Donna!

The next day was Sunday, my usual day off from work. I told myself when I got up that morning, "I have to call Sis today," excited to tell her the news that I could go see her. I wanted to make sure she was doing okay. Even though my life was nothing but work and exhaustion at Christmas time, I had to make the effort to stay in contact with her. I had some chores to get finished and then I would make the call. When I finished my chores I decided to wrap a couple of Christmas gifts and get that out of the way. Days off at that time of year? There was no such thing. We barely had time to take a break at work. My whole body was in constant pain and I felt exhausted. Anything I was normally feeling was magnified times ten. I did my best not to complain and just keep going. It was fast paced at work this time of year and I managed to stay on top somehow.

I always kept my Christmas tags and tape in the top drawer of an antique, oak dresser I have in my spare bedroom. This happens to be where I also store all my photo albums. I opened the top drawer to grab the supplies and I noticed two photos I had laid right on top of a Christmas card box. My plan was to get both photos put together in one frame to give to Donna for Christmas. It was two photos we had taken of each other, holding a rose in our hand that had belonged to our mother. On the photos, we were sitting on the back step of our home when our parents lived in Gander on Gordon Street. She was eighteen and I would have been nineteen in the photos. I had placed them on top of the cards so I would see them when I opened the drawer and I wouldn't forget to get them framed. A feeling came over me when I held them in my hand and as I looked down at them I was thinking, "I have to get them framed for Donna for Christmas." At that very same moment, I heard that gentle voice inside my head quietly say, "She won't be here." I suddenly felt a deep sadness come over me, but I did what I usually do, I shrugged it off. The time would have been somewhere around 1:30 pm.

I placed the photos back in the drawer, grabbed the tape and can of Christmas tags and closed the drawer thinking, "I have to call her as soon as I am finished wrapping these gifts." Little did I know that at that moment that I held those two photos in my hand and had that thought, Donna passed away! I was told an hour later. I think me taking out those two photos and looking at us at such a wonderful time in our life, was what she would have wanted me to remember.

I finished wrapping the gifts, took a phone call from my close friend Beverly, who was in the hospital at the time. I talked to her for about half an hour. I had only just hung up from her about five minutes and my phone rang again. It was Mona's number that showed up on my phone display. I picked up the phone, and Junior's voice was on the other end. I said, "Hello."

He said, "Diane, Donna's gone." Just like that!

I said, "What do you mean?" He was as calm and cool as a stranger, so I didn't dream he meant dead. I heard no emotion whatsoever in his voice. It wasn't registering to me what he was trying to tell me. (Junior was using drugs at that time.)

He said, "She's gone Sis. She died at home." Donna's husband had called them from the hospital. His coolness about it probably added to my anger that came on like a tornado. A whirlwind of emotion erupted inside me!!!

I was instantly flooded with anger. I had always imagined I would be with her if she died before me. "OH NOOO!" I cried.

I lost all control and kept screaming, "NOOOOOOO, NOOOOOO!!!" over and over. I fell to my knees as I clutched the phone! "NOOOOO, NOOOOOOO!!!!" I cried. I wanted to hit something, HARD!!!

Mona told me later she was there with Junior and her best friend Theresa. Theresa went to take the phone from Junior because he didn't know what to do. When Theresa heard me screaming she walked away from the phone, she didn't know what to do either.

I had never felt this kind of intense anger and pain come on this strong and fast in my entire life! Junior asked if I wanted him to drive from Fort McMurray to come get me. I screamed back at him, "NO, I'M NOT COMING UP THERE!!" The anger was so intense I wanted to rip something apart. I was devastated!!!!

Finally I cried "I HAVE TO GO!!" sobbing uncontrollably...I had to process this. All I knew was my Donna was gone, forever!! "WHY DIDN'T I FOLLOW MY INSTINCTS?! OH WHY, OH WHY, OH WHY?! NOW SHE'S GONE, IT'S TOO LATE! THE ANGER, WHAT DO I DO WITH ALL THIS NOW?!!" I cried. I held my hands to my chest trying to stop the intense pain. "I AM SO F***ING ANGRY!!" I was completely out of control. As the minutes passed, overwhelming and complete sadness hit me and my heart broke and I just lay there and sobbed. I needed someone to help me, but I lived here all alone at the time.

I felt my heart was literally breaking out of my chest. I was on the floor, not knowing what to do with myself. I forced myself to get up and I picked up the phone to call my only close friend I had in Edmonton, and that was Beverly, who I had just talked to before my life fell completely apart. I knew she couldn't do anything for me but I was desperate to have someone close to talk to. I dialed the number and Bev picked up the phone.

When I called, I thought I could talk to her but I didn't realize I wouldn't be able to talk properly because of my grief. I would try to be calm because I did not want to upset her, it didn't work out that way. As soon as she answered, I spoke. "Bev my sister died," I sobbed and tried my hardest to speak calmly and clearly.

"Who is this?" she asked.

"It's Diane," I replied. "My sister Donna died," still sobbing and trying to speak properly.

Again, she asked. "Who is this? I can't pick out what you're saying."

I couldn't believe she didn't know it was me. I thought I was speaking clearly. I had just hung up from her no more than fifteen minutes before. "How can she not know it is me?" I thought. Thinking about it later I remembered how I didn't know my own sister's voice when she was distraught. I tried and tried to calm down so she could understand my words. I was mad at myself now because I was upsetting her. Finally I took many deep breaths and talked as slowly and clearly as I could.

I repeated, "Bev it's me, Diane, my sister Donna is gone, she died!"

This time she understood me and she cried, "OH NO!!!" I made her upset and I felt bad after for calling her and doing that. There was nothing she could do for me being in the hospital. It wasn't fair for me to do that. Bev tried to convince me to call her sister Roberta and go there, but I didn't want her family to see me like that. I said, "I will be okay," after I calmed down some. She told me to call my ex-boyfriend who was living in Edmonton at the time. I didn't want to call him, but I promised her I would think about it.

After I hung up talking to Bev, I decided to call my ex Barry. Our last conversation over the phone had not been good and it had been a few weeks since I last spoke to him. I just knew I needed someone with me in that moment who knew how close I was to Donna. Barry had known my family for many years and he knew how close we were. I picked up the phone and dialed his number, he answered. "Hello," he said, I could hear the coldness in his voice. I wanted to hang up right away but I needed his help and I felt we were always there for each other even after we broke up. I tried to stay calm so he could understand me. I told him Donna had passed away. He responded by saying, "that's too bad," still a little cold. He was still mad at me after our last argument, and not even this was moving him. I said "goodbye," to him and hung up. I leaned on the wall and slid back down to the floor. I felt lifeless and I felt completely alone in the world.

No more than ten minutes went by and my buzzer rang. I peeled myself up off the floor and went to answer the buzzer. My legs felt weak. My chest was so tight with grief and I still felt like I wanted to scream but I managed to keep it together.

It was Barry's voice over the intercom, so I buzzed him in. When he came inside my apartment, I was walking in circles like a crazy person, didn't know what to do or where to go. I kept pacing and repeating, "I DON'T KNOW WHAT TO DO, I DON'T KNOW WHAT TO DO!" Over and over I repeated the same thing. "I need my sister!" I sobbed.

I knew Barry still cared about me and would get over his own anger to take care of me. He never liked it when I put him in his place, but he always got over it. Barry is a compulsive gambler and the lying about it caused many problems in our relationship. I would get angry at him any time he lied to me. We never stayed angry at each other; this was probably the longest time. His coldness I am sure came from some of his own denial. I had told him off big time in our last conversation. Forgiveness is something I do easily. That is why we still remain friends to this day. That and the fact that I know he is one of the good ones. If he needed somewhere to stay for a short time when he didn't have his own place, he would call me. We were companions but only that for many years after the break up. I had also helped him out when he was down and out and had nowhere to go but I told him, no more. He had to help himself.

When I tried telling Barry about my last conversation with Donna and how she had wanted me to go there for Christmas, I fell to my knees again. There was so much anger, anguish, pain, regret, guilt, the feelings of just wanting to die and be with her. I was buckled over with the pain, it was so deep! "WHY OH WHY?!!" I cried. "WHY?!" I thought losing my mother was the worst thing I would ever go through, losing my soul mate was far worse for me. This intense pain was horrible and uncontrollable!

Barry got me up off the floor and held me and I sobbed with my last conversation with my sister playing over in my head. When I finally calmed myself enough, we made the decision that I would catch the bus in the morning. "I will stay the night with you and take you to the bus in the morning." he said. He had to work or he would have taken me to Fort McMurray. I was appreciative that he did that. I felt by then his anger at me had left.

I made reservations for the bus when I got up the next morning. I had dozed off somewhere in the early morning, after a hard sleepless night of regret and anguish. I called my work and spoke to my boss, to let her know what happened and that I would be gone for a week or two. Now, I get Christmas off?! My family and I had already buried mom at Christmas time. This was going to be tough!

I called Bev the next morning and apologized for calling her the night before in such a mess. It was a bad move on my part. If she was home and I could have gone there and it would have been different, but she wasn't well and there was nothing she could have done for me. She was very sweet to me and understood.

I was to catch the noon bus. The anger was still pounding at my chest that morning. My chest was so tight, it scared me. I knew I had to do something to try to release some of it or I would have a heart attack, and the best way I knew how to deal with anything emotional, was to write about it.

I sat down and wrote a one page letter to my sister Donna, a "goodbye letter." I don't remember all that I wrote in the letter, but I did express that I had no right to be angry, if anyone did, she did. She suffered so much of her life, having cancer three different times would have been too much for anyone to cope with. Then the addiction to codeine, Hepatitis C, bipolar disorder, osteoporosis, open heart surgery and the side effects from it all was tremendous! The craziest thing about it all was she kept her humor and her quick wit about her through it all. She made everyone around her smile and laugh with her. I had no right to be so angry because I wasn't there with her when she left, I should have been grateful she went peacefully. Donna had every right to go when she did, "she was tired of being sick," she had told me that, and I told her "I understood." I believe she felt her death was near but wouldn't tell me that when I had called her. Why should she have to wait for me to be with her? That was arrogant on my part. It was probably easier on me, not to be with her when she passed, that's why I wasn't there. My heart couldn't have taken it and she knew that. I had to accept this as my answer. Writing always gives me clarity when I need it.

    It was clear to me she had enough. I didn't ever think it would have happened so fast. Donna knew how much I loved her and I believed I would be with her again one day, that gives me a lot of peace and comfort. I said I was sorry in the letter. I wished I had gone to see her when she asked me to and that I loved her and would miss her every day. I finished the letter and I planned on putting it with her in her casket. I had found some peace through my writing. My chest suddenly wasn't tight anymore, I could breathe again. The grief was deep, but the anger I had felt, subsided right away. I believed and accepted her body had finally given up on her but I knew she was with me in spirit, always. Acceptance was key to my sanity!

    I packed the things I would need to take to go to Fort McMurray and remembered to take something to read for the five hour trip. I grabbed the book my boss had given me for Christmas just two days before. I had read the back cover already and knew it was going to be an inspirational, positive read, which I needed right now, but I had no idea how this little book would help with my grief. "Everything happens for a reason."

Diane and Donna. 1976

Chapter Sixteen
Goodbye Sis

It was noon when I got on the bus to Fort McMurray. I was still reeling from the news and now walking in what felt like a fog. I felt spacey and light-headed. My heart hurt, my stomach hurt, everything hurt. I was dreading going there, but I knew I had to face it. One of the hardest things I ever had to do in my life! I had my new book with me, hopefully it would distract me even briefly, and hopefully it would teach me something.

When I look back on how every little thing happens, I believe more and more that yes we have free will, but I believe every choice we make is the one we are supposed to make to teach us something important.

I would try to read to take my mind off the whirlwind I felt I was now in. I didn't think I would be able to focus on the words but I would try. Who knew that it would turn out to be exactly what I needed to read at that time?! I had the letter that I had written to my sister in my purse, and I had packed enough clothes to last me a week. I hoped I wouldn't be there any longer than that. The pressure of getting back to work was on me for sure, but for now I had to focus on my sister and my family.

There had been no word on how Donna had passed yet and wouldn't be for a while. I was grateful that she hadn't suffered a horrible dragged out death. That much she deserved, after all the suffering she had been through in her lifetime. Who would have my back and love me unconditionally now? That was a selfish thought but there it was. She was the one that told me constantly that she was proud of me. The tears fall when I remember this...no one would ever care about me as much as she did. My kids do of course but it is a different kind of love. In my immediate family, Donna was the one person in my life that never passed any judgment in anything I chose to do, just total support and praise. That kind of adult connection is rare and I would miss it so much. I needed this to be a bad dream that I could wake up from at any moment. But reality would set in soon enough. I had four siblings and each one of us had a different relationship with each other. I was definitely on the same page as Donna. I loved her and was just as proud of her. I bragged about her many talents to everyone I knew. She was a protective mom who took good care of and loved her three children that she raised. She would cook many, big family meals over the years that were always delicious! She did many crafts with her children when they were younger. I remember specifically her making chocolate candy in these little candy molds. We always had fun at her home doing that as a family. Donna was very artistic and she loved to do flower arrangements and worked at a flower shop for some time at the Peter Pond Mall in Fort McMurray. She did great drawings when we were teenagers. She made the best pineapple squares money could buy. She was known for them. She was a great singer and sang beautiful harmony. She could pick up any instrument and play it by ear. She was also the best friend anyone could ask for. Perfect? No, nobody is perfect but she was perfect to me.

    I was lucky to have a single seat on the bus this time of year with such short notice, but because it was the beginning of the week it wasn't full. I had my pillow with me, I held it on my lap, pulling it close to my stomach to stifle the deep pain I felt and the screams I wanted to release when it would get overwhelming. I couldn't do that here. I had to hold it in. Pressing my pillow to my stomach helped tremendously, but the silent tears still quietly trickled down my face. I took out my book and started reading it. As I read each chapter, I was quite surprised at how this book talked about many of the things I needed at this very moment. It even had a part of a chapter telling you how you should grieve. Really?! I was amazed by this! I needed all the help I could get to get me through this. I finished the book by the time I arrived in Fort McMurray. It was remarkable how much this wonderful book would help me manage to get through the next few months. I had skimmed through a lot of it and would re-read it again at a later time. I really focused on the part about "grief." Never in my life did I need "Don Miguel Riuz" words as much as I did at that exact time. Without this book, I know the whole process of losing a soul mate would have been much harder on me and I don't know if I would have ever got past the deep grief as well as I did. I am very grateful to my ex-boss Patty for "The Four Agreements." To think I received it as a gift the day before Donna's death was no coincidence in my mind.

  When I arrived at the drop off point in Fort McMurray, there was no one there to pick me up from the bus. I waited 10 minutes and then took a cab to Mona's home where I would be staying. Junior was there and said "I went to get you but I thought you had already arrived and somehow I missed you." There was still no emotion from him. I could see he was clearly stoned. I felt the old resentment right away. He was floating through this and I had to feel everything. It didn't seem fair somehow. Then I caught myself and thought, "Who am I to judge someone else's pain, their strengths and weaknesses and how they deal with things?" I had to let it go and deal with why I was there. I did feel compassion for my brother but it was sometimes difficult.

I knew it was important for my own sanity and health down the road to let myself feel it all. Reading and learning has given me the knowledge that has helped me tremendously in dealing with many things in my life and now knowing how to help this process of grief, was priceless knowledge that would help me. I know everyone deals with loss in their own way, but I was going to use what I had just learned. One thing I knew for certain, bottling up pain kills people every day, in every way. I wasn't about to do that.

The reunion was tearful between Mona and me. We just held each other for a while and cried. Theresa was there at Mona's and she came and hugged me. We all sat at the kitchen table and talked and cried. I got more details on how Donna's husband had been napping in their bedroom and woke up to find her sleeping, he had thought, in her lazy boy in their living room. When he realized she wouldn't wake up, he called an ambulance. That was about all we knew. I know that the chances of most people being with their loved ones while passing is rare and I know, that she knew, there was nothing I wouldn't do for her if I could. I had found some kind of peace with that thought. If I had to call everyone every time I worried about my sister over the years, it would have been a full time job. I knew her well enough that she would forgive me for not taking the time off to go see her right away and more importantly I had forgiven myself! I was still carrying some guilt that I kept putting off calling her on the day she passed and focused so much on getting my chores done first. I knew in time, this would pass too. I believe when God wants us, there is nothing we can do to change it. Could have, should have, can drive us crazy if we let it.

Junior was staying in contact with Donna's husband at the hospital. We were told there was no point in going to the hospital. We could not see her yet. I wanted to see her, but yet dreading it at the same time.

The next couple of days were busy. There were messages to take and preparing for her service. Her children and husband wanted her service to be at the Gospel Church, and Mona and I were fine with that. Junior was not. We were told, "because of her age, there had to be an autopsy." I called work to let my boss know I would have to take another week off work.

The arguments between Junior and Mona were numerous because he was using. My goal was to try and stay out of it while I was there. I did not want any part of the drama and now here I was, smack dab in the middle of it again during my sister's memorial preparations. My mother's funeral was the same with some family members. Dealing with the loss of a loved one should have been enough to deal with. It was times like this where I felt stuck. Although I needed to be with my family, I would have stayed at a hotel if it weren't so expensive. All I prayed for was to get through it all, pay my respects to my sister and to go home.

The time had finally been set to go see my sister at the funeral home. We were told there was a meeting at 10 a.m. and we needed to be there by then. It was to arrange the memorial service and for the family viewing. Finally, I would see my sister. I felt sick to my stomach!

Mona, Junior and I had picked out two of the four songs they needed, that we thought the whole family might agree on for the service. My father's song "Home by the Sea," which was Donna's favorite of his, and "Silent Night," which was her favorite Christmas carol.

When we arrived at the funeral home, I felt anxious and dread. I was so torn. My feelings were all over the place. Mona asked Donna's husband if we could pick out something for Donna to wear and was told "yes." We had gone and bought a nice black dress jacket for Donna to wear, assuming there would be a normal viewing. Her husband and immediate family were taking care of things and we would do what we were asked and was respectful to their own grief. I wanted Donna to wear a blouse that I owned and I knew she would have loved underneath the jacket. I felt everyone was okay with it. It was a very pretty purple, black and pink patterned top, made of silk. Donna had very feminine taste and I knew she would have loved the vibrant colors. When her family was called into the meeting, we were not invited. Mona, Junior and I just looked at each other and left it alone. I just needed to see my sister to know that she was at peace. What I got was a very different experience!

The viewing started and Donna's children went in first as did her husband. My heart broke for them. I knew how hard it was to lose your Mom. When they finished the viewing and came back out, they were clearly heartbroken! It was our turn to go in the viewing room. My stomach was in knots and I started to feel even more anxiety building up in my chest. I remembered the five words from the book I had read "Don't hold in your grief." When we stepped just a little inside past the doorway, I caught a glimpse of my sister lying on a gurney to my left. I cried out and went to my knees!! Junior and Mona were holding me up. This was too painful for me to even try and hold in. There was no controlling it, it was a horrible feeling! When I pulled myself together enough to walk, I took the dreaded steps towards where my sister was lying.

Never did I expect to see my sister laid out on a gurney with a sheet pulled up to her neck. As we came closer to her lying there I was horrified!! There was no coffin, no make-up, and no smile that the professionals usually painted on loved ones faces to make our loved ones look at peace. I couldn't believe what I was seeing! "My poor sister!" was all I could think. I was heartbroken and angry again! This was totally unexpected. They had brushed out her long soft grey, blonde hair and that was it. "Why is she looking like this?" I cried. I would have this last picture of her in my head forever. Nobody would answer my questions. Nobody offered to take us aside or take us to the office to explain. The people that worked there should certainly know! I was so upset! Mona and Junior were on each side of me and we just held each other. It was terrible! Nothing like the beautiful viewing my mother had. I was so heartbroken for my sister!

    After a few minutes and trying to get past the initial shock, I calmed myself down and just wept, shaking my head in grief and sadness. She deserved better! The letter I had written for her I laid by her side and we left shortly after. I calmed down when we walked out of the viewing room. My children had showed up and I was glad to see them. I was also grateful they were not there to see me at the beginning of the viewing. My daughters hugged me tight. Hanna was already in tears. Jeanna said, "Mom, I feel a big lump in my throat." I said, "Jeanna, you need to cry, it's okay." My sweet girl who held everything inside worried me. After a while she laid her head on my shoulder and I saw the tears. This moved me even more. I rarely saw my oldest daughter cry.

    After we all left and went home, I kept talking to Mona and questioning why she thought our sister was looking like that and mostly why she was on a gurney instead of a casket? She didn't understand it either but wasn't making the fuss about it that I was. It bothered me enough that I called the funeral home two days later and put the question to them. The woman I talked to

GOODBYE SIS

response was, "they could only do so much with her body because she was having an autopsy." At least some things made sense to me now, but it was a final picture that will never leave my mind. I understood a little more after the phone call. I didn't want to upset her children any more than they already were by asking too many questions. My experience with funerals/memorials so far has been, not wanting to rock the boat, because everyone is already highly emotional. Losing someone we love is hard enough. Donna's husband dropped by Mona's and gave me $200 from Donna's money to help with my expenses. I didn't want to take it and politely said no, but our friend who was there at the time wasn't having it. She came over to me, leaned into my ear and said, "That's Donna's money and she would want you to have it so you take it!" I just wanted my sister back, not her money but the gesture was appreciated and I accepted it.

The memorial service didn't take place until two weeks after I had arrived in Fort McMurray. The church was beautiful and still had Christmas trees lit up. I felt like I wanted to run the moment I entered the gathering room. I looked inside and saw my sister's urn with her ashes in it, sitting on a table with her picture and a lot of beautiful flower arrangements around her. My family had ordered two dozen pink roses. I checked to see if they were there and they were. They were beautifully arranged, as were all the flowers.

I moved closer to the alter and I reached out and touched the cold surface of the urn, and the tears flowed. I looked at her photo and it felt like someone grabbed my heart and squeezed it tight. I remember thinking the words "don't leave me Sis, please don't leave me." Those words ran through my head many times that day. Anyone that knew my sister Donna loved her. I still felt like I was floating sometimes, like I was in a dream that I was about to wake up from. A couple of people came inside the church and hugged me as I stood there. I said a few words to my sister in my mind, knowing she was there in spirit and could hear me. I pulled myself away to walk out and join the other family members gathered inside another room. I greeted some friends I had not seen for a long time who were waiting in the lobby. I painted on my smile, as my heart ached.

When the service started, the Pastor and my family walked down the aisle of the church where there were friends and family already gathered and waiting. The Pastor led our group. Donna's children and husband walked behind the Pastor. Mona, myself and our children were right behind them. My two daughters were on each side of me, arm in arm. I had no idea where my brother went. The further we walked down the aisle, the more overwhelmed I was feeling. There it was again….that feeling of wanting to run, and it was powerful this time! I suddenly tried pulling away briefly and quietly whimpered, "no." Both my daughters and Mona stopped in their tracks just for a second and they looked at me. I said nothing, just continued on. "I can do this," I told myself, "I can do this!"

There were lots of family photos in a slide show that pulled on my heart strings, and they did play my father's song we requested. The eulogy I wrote from myself and our family was read by her daughter-in-law and the personal messages were read. The service was soon over and I was more than ready to leave and go home.

The next day I was back on the bus to Edmonton, exhausted. I was very pleasantly surprised to see a friend get on the bus last minute. Breda Kavanagh is a sweet Irish lady who was one of Donna's best friends over the years that we lived in Fort McMurray. Breda sat with me on the trip back to Edmonton. I was very happy she was there. It made for a much more pleasant five hour drive. She had been at Donna's memorial service as well as her adult children. We all did so much together with our families over the years and we had lots to catch up on.

I had let myself grieve my heart out and now, even though I was still under the cloud, I could hopefully start the long road back to healing. I grieved for my sister for the first year after she was gone. The reason why I know I was grieving that long was because it took me that long to be able to talk about her openly without crying. Grief is a different experience for everyone.

I always try and remember my favorite proverb, "This too will pass." And somehow it does!

Chapter Seventeen

Messages from Heaven

After I returned home from Donna's memorial service, I went back to work two days later. I needed to keep busy, that feeling of falling was close by and I knew I was once again battling against the ever- looming anxiety and the attacks that could come with it. I had to keep it under control. I did plenty of journaling and reading positive books. I had several signs from Donna that she was still with me. To remember them even now, eight years later, still makes me emotional as I write about it. I miss her so much.

A month after I returned to work, I went outside on my break. It was a beautiful, sunny February day. It was warm enough outside that I didn't need to wear a coat. As I stood there looking up at the sky, I said in my mind, "Are you with me Sis?"

After a few minutes of gazing at the sky I went back inside and as I took the corner to go inside my store, I saw there was a lady standing at the diamond counter but no one was serving her yet. She had long blondish grey hair and was close to my age with a sweet smile. I said hello to her, and went around the counter to serve her. I asked "can I help you?"

"Yes," she replied. "I am doing some pre shopping for my nephew who is going to be purchasing an engagement ring in the near future."

"Well, let's take a look," I replied as I unlocked the showcase she was standing at. I liked her right away. She had a sweet disposition about her.

I showed her many rings and it was a very relaxed and pleasant experience. I felt like I'd known her forever and we chatted with ease. When we were finished looking at rings, I said, "Let me grab one of my cards for you to give your nephew." I went around to the till area to grab my card from the little card holder. As I was walking back towards her I thought to myself. I have to ask her name. Something I usually would do before now. Right away I heard the soft whisper of the name "Donna," in my head. I ignored it and as I stood in front of the lady and passed her my card, I asked her name? "Donna" she replied. I felt a shiver up my spine! I acted as cool as I could. I said, "Oh, I 'have' a sister named Donna." I didn't want to use the past tense. Looking at my name tag she smiled and replied. "Oh, and I have a sister named Diane." I nearly fell over!!

I kept smiling and looked over at my boss who was standing near and had been listening to the conversation. She didn't know the question I had asked my sister when I was standing outside a few minutes before, or that I had heard the name "Donna," in my head just seconds before I had asked the lady her name. We said our friendly goodbyes, and I did my best not to tear up. Donna left the store. I felt like I wanted to hug her but I knew it would require a teary explanation and make the lady uncomfortable. My boss looked at me and said, "I have goose bumps." When I tearfully filled her in on the rest of the encounter, she cried too. "It was your sister's way of answering your question, and letting you know she is still with you." she said. I agreed. It was pretty incredible to me. I had a smile in my heart and on my face for the rest of the day! Even now when I write about it, years later, it still brings me to happy tears.

It took me three months to finally get up the nerve to listen to the Celine Dion cd that my coworker Dan had given me for Christmas the day before Donna passed away. It was going to be hard to play the cd but it was my day off and I felt I was ready to do it. I wouldn't let my thoughts and memories about my sister go too deep up until now. Anytime I would remember anything about us, I would put it out of my mind quickly, too painful to go there. This day I wanted to relax and let myself remember the last time I was with her at the concert that was so special for us. I was ready and willing to go there now in my mind and in my heart. I missed her terribly and needed the memories. I knew I needed to allow myself to remember her on a deeper level and I expected she would be right there with me.

I was alone in my apartment and I placed the cd in my stereo and lay back in my lazy boy, closed my eyes and relaxed. Every song that played squeezed at my heartstrings and made me tear up as I went deeper into the memories. I let myself picture everything from that last evening with us sitting together at the Celine concert, looking at each other smiling with every new song Celine sang. I pictured it all, the lights, the crowd, and the dancers, everything I could imagine! When "The Power of Love" started to play on my stereo, I went even deeper into my thoughts and remembered how emotional it was for us both, to the point of me tearing up from the memory. I remembered Donna's face as we both looked at each other and smiled when Celine started to sing. I let myself feel everything, how I felt in that very moment and how special it was to share it with someone I had such an emotional bond with. How we understood each other with just a look. It had been a "dream come true," for both of us. I let the music and my memories bring me there!

In that very moment I heard a loud clanging sound come from my kitchen sink. My sink was 7 feet away from where I was sitting. I didn't freak out. I had expected something to happen. I believed Donna would give me a sign. It did give me a jolt because of how loud it sounded in my tiny apartment, even over the music. My heart was racing. I kept my eyes closed; calmed myself down to slow my heart rate and smiled to myself while I finished listening to the song. I was a little scared at first but also as excited as I could be because I knew my sister was there with me at that very moment remembering the concert with me. She was seeing and feeling what I was, and she let me know she was with me experiencing that same memory. The spirit world is something that I can't explain but I find it fascinating!

After the song finished playing, I got up to go look into the kitchen sink to see if I could find where the loud clang sound came from. Not always did I find physical evidence from these spiritual signs, but there it was in my kitchen sink. The plate and mug that I placed in my sink the same way that morning and every morning for countless years after eating my breakfast had been moved. The mug was now tipped over and lying sideways on the plate. Not upright like I had set it down in the sink earlier. I always placed it upright in the center of my plate. The sound I had heard was more of someone throwing a butter knife in the sink than glass on glass, but there it was. There were no other dishes and no cutlery in the sink. I was a little nervous and the hair stood up on my arms. The evidence was right in front of me, and now in my heart. It thrilled me that Donna had joined me in my memory of us!

I believe our loved ones spirit is around us whenever we think of them or need them. The deeper we think of them, the stronger their presence. Believing this gives me great comfort. The proof was undeniable!

None of my family knew for certain what Donna died from. There were two different reports from the autopsy. The first one said "an infection around her heart valve that had been replaced one year before." The second one a couple of months later said it was "suicide from an overdose." Although my sister was depressed in my last conversation with her and I believed she was giving up on life, I didn't believe for a minute she would ever commit suicide. Accidental death maybe, if she started using pain meds again, her body not being used to the large doses anymore. Donna was pleased when I told her I would try and go see her after Christmas. Yes, she was depressed and was tired of being sick but she had been that way countless times before. I believe because she was sick for so much of her life, there were many assumptions made when she died. If I believed my sister overdosed to take her own life, I would have no problem saying it. It may not be right, but I would understand, considering her life of pain and numerous illnesses. I knew her better than anyone and she would never have done that without at least leaving a note for her children. It was also against her beliefs. She finally had the money from her settlement to take a trip back home to Gander when the weather warmed up, something she had dreamed of and looked forward to. I believe they got it wrong! The first report of heart infection and failure made more sense to me. Whether it was her heart or accidental death, I do believe she is at peace.

  I went for a reading with our well known psychic here in Edmonton six months after Donna passed. I have been doing that after the last three deaths of family members. It helps me find peace somehow. Before I left my apartment to go see Paul, I said to Donna in my mind, "I know you will show up Sis and I know you will be the first thing he talks about." Well sure enough, as soon as the reading started he asked if I had recently lost a daughter or sister. I said "Yes, a sister." He said "she passed from the chest area." He went on to say he felt the pain in his chest. I said, "Yes, she had heart problems." I felt peace in hearing what I already believed. Paul said, "She has a message for you. Don't be afraid when you cross over." Through my tears I smiled!

  Thank you Sis! RIP, I love you!

Donna. 2006

Chapter Eighteen
Going Back Home

One of the things my sisters and I wanted to do for many years was to go back to Newfoundland. The last trip we had gone back home together was in the early eighties. For a few years before Donna passed, we talked often of going home together on a vacation. Our children were all grown and we wanted to take the trip together.

By the time Donna had received her payment for the Hepatitis C, it was already getting too cold to go. We all agreed we wanted to go back east in the summertime and we had been elated it might finally happen. I believe it would have been a fantastic trip, but it was a dream that was never meant to happen, at least not with all of us together. I had not been home for seventeen years. Now I would have to go without Donna, I was very sad about that. A line from a John Lennon song comes to mind. "Life is what happens when you're busy making plans."

Donna had told us she wanted her ashes spread on the shores of the river in Clarke's Head, the place we loved so much. I decided to stop putting it off and to go back the summer after she passed, and I did. I felt nothing could stop me from going home in 2009, and even though I couldn't take her ashes with me, because her daughter and Mona wanted to wait and do it at a later date, I went anyways. I was tired of putting it off and now that Donna was gone, I felt I should still make the trip carrying her with me in my heart. I was doing the trip for both of us!

I didn't want to fly on a plane alone because I had great anxiety when I had flown the last time. I was terrified of flying but I was determined to overcome it. I felt if I had someone else to go with me, I would be okay. My constant support, and my closest friend Colette Ulliac who lives in Fort McMurray, decided to go with me. I met Colette nineteen years ago when I found my first job in the Jewelry business at the Peter Pond Mall. We met the second week after we both started our new jobs and we have loved each other ever since. She is another one of my soul sisters. She is the friend that I know is there for me always, even though we rarely see each other anymore since I moved away, but we still talk on the phone on a regular basis to catch up.

I had been talking to Colette back in 2009 and was frustrated that I might have to wait another year to go back home because Mona wanted to wait. I had been waiting seventeen years with every year someone not being able to go. I felt now was the time. My concern was, especially after losing Donna, that I may not make it home either if I kept putting it off. Losing someone you love makes you very aware of your own mortality. I knew it would never be the same going home without my sisters, but I had a sudden desire to not put it off any longer. Colette offered to go with me. I couldn't believe it. I was so excited and grateful! We both had enough air miles to fly back, so how could I refuse! Our flights were booked soon after and I called my dad, very excited to be going home. He wanted to know the dates we would be going so he could book off his holidays for the same time. I let him know that Mona had backed out and I would still be coming with my friend. I knew my family would all love Colette. I didn't think there would be any problems. Seventeen years and finally going home! I was beyond thrilled! I had not taken a vacation in many years and it was much needed. There was sadness that my sisters were not going but Colette was like a sister and I was excited this was happening with her.

We were booked for the beginning of September, my favorite time of the year and Colette and I were taking our first trip together as friends. We got along great so I wasn't worried about anything. My disappointment came the day before we were leaving. I called my dad to confirm when we were leaving and what time we were arriving there. He casually mentioned to me he didn't take any holidays, he had cancelled them. My heart sank and I was speechless! Dad went on to tell me the reason why, one of the guys was off with a broken arm. I felt there were other reasons; Mona not going with me was one. I felt like I was kicked in the stomach! Seventeen years since I had gone home and eight since I saw my father. I was disheartened to say the least.

I contemplated cancelling the trip when I hung up. I called Colette heartbroken and we discussed it. In the end we decided to still go. The main reason I was travelling that far was to spend time with my father. I was disappointed but I knew there were many other family members I wanted to see as well. I had to suck it up and make the best of it. I was going home and I was still excited but now with a heavy heart too.

When Colette and I boarded the plane early morning in Edmonton, I had my private talk to my sister Donna. I had hoped and prayed she would be with me on this trip. I already knew this trip was in honor of her and I whispered to her to stay with me on the trip and take away my fears. She certainly did that and more. I have never felt such peace as I did in those following ten days. We got off the plane in Gander at midnight and I literally kneeled to kiss the ground, I was so happy! Colette and I rented a SUV and we were off to the Hotel. Family had offered for us to stay with them, but I have so many allergies, I felt less stress for me and them by staying at a hotel. It also gave us the freedom to get up and go whenever we wanted without disturbing anyone.

The next day I was so excited to go and finally see my family. It was thrilling to be home! I tried my hardest not to feel any resentment towards my father and was still very excited to see him, but the hurt was still lingering and I felt it the whole trip. I was fifty three now, 17 years older than the last time I was home and I had been through many changes since that last time. There was a lot I realized about my family dynamics when I was on that trip. I was not that scared little girl anymore, was the main thing.

My mother's family had a gathering for us at my Grandmother Peckford's homestead. Uncle Tom and Aunt Marie now live in that home and Uncle Tom did a wonderful job renovating it and bringing it back to life. What a terrific weekend we had of great music and laughter with my family and friends. I got to play guitar and sing in front of my family for the first time. The delicious food brought back sweet memories of home for me. My Aunts, Jeanette, Betty, Joan and Roz were there as were my Uncles, Tom, Cliff, Paul, Randy, Hubert and family and friends Glenis, Faith and Doug. I missed my father being there but he was working.

I got to walk on the beach again as I did so many times as a young girl with my siblings. The memories came flooding back as I sat on a boulder, looked out over the water. The smell of the salt air was refreshing and I could suddenly breathe deep, with no effort. I could have stayed in that moment forever. Colette was getting along famously with everyone and she walked on the beach with me along with my Aunt Roz and Uncle Paul. I was thinking about Donna the whole time, wishing she was there, along with the rest of my family who I missed dearly. There were so many fond memories for me. It was on a trip to Fogo Island the following week when Donna let me know she was definitely with me!

Myself, Colette, my father, my Aunt Ruby (dad's sister), and my cousin Brian decided to take the trip to Fogo Island where my grandfather, Stanley Waterman was born and raised. Dad finally had three days off and this was when I would get to spend some quality time with him. We had to drive about an hour from Glenwood after we picked up my Aunt and Brian, and were on our way to catch the ferry that crossed at lunch time. When we got to the dock there was a small lineup of about seven or eight cars, so we took our place in line. As we sat there waiting, I said to my father I was a little nervous about driving the SUV onto the ferry. He said, "I will do it." I got out of the driver's seat and sat in the back directly behind him. I had a terrible fear of boats and had not been on the water for twenty years, but strangely I was feeling fairly relaxed about it. As we sat there, again for the hundredth time during my trip, I thought of Donna. She would have loved to take the ferry and go to the island we visited so many years before. For the first time on the trip I asked her a question. "Sis, are you with me?" I also thought, "How could she possibly give me a sign with us just sitting here in a vehicle?" It seemed impossible. That very second my cousin Brian said "What's going on there?" I turned my head from staring out the side window and said "What?" He pointed to the light fixture on the ceiling over his head. The light fixture had two divided little square covers, in the center of the ceiling. The one on the left closest to where I was sitting had come on. No one had touched it. I smiled to myself grinning from ear to ear and thought, if I tell them what I had just asked two seconds before this happened, no one would believe me. I did tell them "I had just asked Donna if she was with me" and no one said a word. Awkward... but I couldn't stop smiling. I know it was probably because Dad was there why no one responded. The rest of us were believers, but my dad was not, at the time. No one wanted to 'rock the boat' so to speak. I was overjoyed that yes indeed, I had just received confirmation that my sister was with me on this trip in spirit. I had already felt that she was there because it was such a peaceful trip for me. All anxiety I had been feeling for decades had left me completely.

When we finally drove onto the ferry, we had to leave our vehicles and go to the top deck. I had a deathly fear of heights and water, so again, I worried for a few seconds but then I was not feeling any real fear. It almost felt weird. It was not normal for me to not feel some amount of anxiety. Back then I was still learning how to get my fears and anxiety under control. This was so easy it felt strange to me. I didn't have to work at it.

It was a beautiful sunny day and the water was rippling but calm. We climbed to the top deck and as we got out in the deeper water, I was standing looking around at all the sparkles coming off the water from the sunlight hitting it. I suddenly felt overwhelmed, like an out of body experience and I couldn't catch a breath. I broke down crying from the sheer beauty of it all and I reached out for Colette who was standing next to me. I gasped and said, "She is with me, I can feel her," through my sob. Colette knew what I meant right away and grabbed my hand to help me sit on a bench. "Yes," she said, "your sister is with you, most definitely!" I felt such peace, but yet so much emotion, it was indescribable. All my fears had left me and as I let the tears roll down my cheeks for a moment, all I saw was the beauty that surrounded me and I felt Donna was seeing it too, through my eyes. It was an incredible feeling!

I walked around freely after that, even leaning out over the railing to gaze at the water and all the beautiful surroundings. To also have my father standing right next to me was great! It was a wonderful feeling of freedom, to feel no fear. I was "in the moment," fully! I felt I had done my duty as her sister and carried her home with me. Donna was there enjoying it all as I was, I felt she was seeing and feeling everything through me and she had let me know she was.

It was a trip of a lifetime and I will never forget those ten days with my sister (in spirit), my family and my friend and soul sister, Colette. Thank you for going with me Colette. It meant the world to me to have you on the best trip I have ever experienced to date!

The last night we were there, my father, Colette and I drove from Gander to have supper at my Aunt Ruby's home in Glenwood. She had cooked a wonderful turkey supper for us, as did my Aunt Roz the week before. We were blessed to have a "cooked feed" twice while we were there. It was all delicious! Spending this time with my friend and family was precious to me.

On our way driving back to Gander that last evening, there was a light rain falling. We saw there was a double rainbow right ahead of us. It was the first rain we had in the ten days we were there. I gasped when I saw the double rainbow, and we stopped on the side of the road to take a picture of it. It was spectacular and I couldn't think of a better way to have ended such a wonderful trip. I don't need or long to go anywhere else in the world as long as I can go back to Newfoundland again. God willing!

Me and Dad. 2009

Chapter Nineteen

My Friend Beverly

Two years after Donna passed away my best friend here in Edmonton, Beverly, became very ill and was taken to emergency. She had many health issues for many years after a surgery that had complications. Now she was down with a terrible flu. Again, it was Christmas time. I considered Bev to be like another soul sister to me. We had a very special connection.

The hospital kept her in and placed her in ICU. I was very worried about her because she was so sick. I hoped and prayed that she would be okay. I went to visit her at the hospital a few times over the course of a few days. On Boxing Day afternoon, I was getting myself ready to go see her again. I was in my bedroom getting dressed and I opened the pewter jewelry box that I keep on my dresser. It was a Christmas gift I had given to Donna. Her name is engraved on the lid. It was where I keep some of my earrings as well. It also held a little, heart shaped tin with Donna's ashes in it. When I opened the lid to get a pair of earrings, I looked at the heart shape tin and picked it up, kissed it and said "Merry Christmas Sis." I put the little tin back inside the box, grabbed the earrings and closed the lid. I went to the closet to grab my sweater off the hanger that I was going to wear to the hospital. It was a cold and cloudy day, and I wanted to be warm. When I pulled the grey and white, cowl neck sweater off the hanger, something hit the floor right next to where I was standing. I looked down squinting at the floor but couldn't really see what it was until I bent down closer. I had taken my glasses off to pull the sweater over my head. It was a silver brooch that Donna had given to me when she had open heart surgery. It was shaped like a Calla Lily flower and had pink crystals in it. I got goose bumps to see it now laying on the floor right next to me! I also realized in that moment, that the pink jacket that I wore this brooch on was in the other bedroom hanging in the closet there. I never removed it off that jacket. I only kept pants and sweaters in this end of my main bedroom closet. Tops were on the other side and dressy clothes for work I kept in the spare room. I could feel the goose bumps from head to toe! I stared at this beautiful brooch I now held in my hand in wonderment. It should have been in the next room, pinned to my pink jacket. Now it was flying out of the closet five seconds after I kissed her little can of ashes and I wished her a Merry Christmas? Wow! "How can a spirit possibly do that?" I tried to figure out anyway possible it could have moved to where my jeans and sweaters were, but it was impossible. That sweater was never hung close to that jacket. I could now picture my sister Donna, with her impish grin on her face. I shook my head, smiled and continued to get ready to leave for the hospital.

  I was in denial that Bev could possibly pass away anytime soon, especially that same night. I didn't want to believe it was possible. When I arrived at the hospital that day, she was already in a coma state. I went in her room, and there was another lady friend of hers there. I began to weep when I looked at her lifeless body in the bed. She had no life in her at all now. "Don't cry," her friend said to me firmly. I ignored it. I went to Bev's bedside to see her, making small talk to her friend. I was uncomfortable so I left the room and went downstairs. I went back up awhile later and her other friend had left. I was glad to have alone time with Bev and I talked to her believing she could hear me. A wonderful nurse came in and saw I was tearful. She motioned me to the other side of the room and took the time to sit with me and talk to me. "It's not good is it?" I asked.

She replied, "No, it's not."

"There is hope though." I said.

She said, "There is always hope."

When the nurse left the room I watched my beautiful friend sleep and leaned over her to whisper a few last words in her ear. I told her how much I loved her and then kissed her and left.

Beverly passed away later that night surrounded by her loved ones. Her sister Roberta was with her, her brother Del, her beautiful niece Courtney and sweet nephew Jordan. This family means the world to me and was my family when I was living here all alone for 6 years.

I wondered after I got the call the next day that Bev had passed, if my sister Donna already knew I was going to lose my friend that night? I wondered if Donna was letting me know the day before with the brooch that she was watching over me and was supporting me, like always. I feel my sister Donna and my soul sister Beverly are always watching over me. I don't doubt that they are friends in the spirit world. They were very much alike.

To lose another "sister" was devastating for me. Bev had the most electric, bright, beautiful smile that I have ever seen and a very warm heart. All my children who had met her said right away, "She reminds me of Aunt Donna." Bev had the best laugh where her head would go back and her body would shake with laughter, with not a sound coming out of her. Both of us were soft hearted and loved to laugh, so we got along well. She knew she could call me for anything and I felt the same way about her. I could share anything with her and she would not judge me. That same feeling I shared with my sister Donna. I believe Bev and I were meant to meet when I desperately needed a good friend. My heart was broken when she died and I would miss her terribly! She had been the first person I had called when Donna passed away and now she was gone too.

I did get a sign from Beverly a few days after she passed that she was around me in spirit. I was sitting in my spare room where I had a shelf with books and a few decorative ornaments on it. I have a glass lady ornament that you can turn the bottom and it plays the song, "You light up my life." It is a birthday gift I received from my friend Betty Sanders many years ago. I was sitting and letting myself think of Bev intensely, knowing that if she was around me, I would probably get a sign. What is amazing is you never know what the sign will be. Suddenly I heard one note play from the glass lady and I knew right away from the sound what it was, without turning to look. I let myself relax, calm my heart from racing and just sat still and listened. It happened four more times, just one note at a time and it would stop. I smiled with tears in my eyes and said. "I know you're here Bev, I love you and miss you too."

I have had that ornament for thirty years. It never started playing on its own, before or since, it only happened on that day that I needed to know if Bev was still near me. Our bond was real and strong, and I will miss her forever.

RIP Beverly! I love you.

Chapter Twenty
Surprise Arrival

When the phone rang that September day in 2011, I hesitated to pick it up. I had talked to my dad the day before, and he had told me my sister Mona had left on the bus from Fort McMurray to move to Edmonton. She had not called me or told me anything about it. My anxiety went through the roof right away. "Oh my God," I thought to myself. "This will be the end of me!" I had lost my Mom and had gone through a scary divorce. Just as I thought I was getting some peace from a two year struggle with my son and the loss of Donna and then Beverly, Mona was going to be at my doorstep looking to move in with me at any moment. It seemed I wasn't going to get a break for long!

    I was already struggling on a daily basis with my own health. The pain I had from fibromyalgia almost daily was enough to deal with. Just when the clouds seem to part again, here comes my chain smoking, gambling addicted, negative thinking sister, who I loved but struggled to get along with. This would surely finish me off. She would be bringing with her all her problems along with everyone else's and without a doubt, she would be broke. I know she may not be happy with me right now in spirit, but hopefully she will be by the time I get to the end of our story. The one thing that annoyed her most about me was my openness because she was more tightly lipped about herself.

My mental and physical health, I take very seriously. I felt anxious sometimes when I was with her, the same feeling I got around my father sometimes. I would pick up on the angry energy she carried with her. Yes, we clashed many times over the years about many topics and on many levels. We were polar opposites in many ways. I did admire some of the traits Mona had that I and my other siblings didn't have. The fact that she could take a tremendous amount of stress was amazing to me. She seemed to thrive on it at times. Being able to keep things to herself may have been a good trait to some people. Just because we didn't agree on most things, doesn't mean either of us was wrong, we just had very different opinions about life in general.

My sister also loved the phone. My father would jokingly say whenever our family needed to call anyone, "get Mona to call, she loves the phone." Mona was the one that stayed in contact with the whole family over the years. She was far better at it than me or any other family member. This was where she shined and was appreciated. Her memory was very sharp. She could remember every family member's birthday, including extended family members and friends. She could also remember anyone's phone number from years ago. If we needed to get information on anything in the family, we would ask Mona. Again, she was very much like Dad in that way. His memory was amazing. Yet anything uncomfortable, they had no memory of. Mona was constantly phoning our family and our friends over the years, filling the rest of us in on what was going on with everyone in the family. I am very grateful for this now and I know I could never fill her footsteps in that area. I am not a phone person at all. I call my kids on a regular basis and a couple of family and friends once and awhile, that's it.

Mona had a quick wit. She had a fun side that could crack us up when she was happy. I rarely saw that side of her anymore and I missed it. I believe we all inherited our quick wit from our mother. She made our father laugh often with her sassy come backs.

I had just started to receive unemployment in August after waiting for months. How in the world was I going to support the two of us now on $650 every two weeks? As good as I am with money this was going to be a huge challenge, considering my sister spent about $1000 a month on cigarettes alone. Mona smoked a minimum of two packs a day and when she was stressed, three easily. I was a little ticked at my oldest sister to tell the truth. How dare she spend a ton of money gambling and then come to my doorstep when she was broke. It was about to happen, I could feel it in my bones! Mona was receiving a monthly allowance of $800 from her ex. At least that was something to hopefully help her get a place but it would only cover her rent, not even her cigarettes. I had to stay positive as much as possible. The worrying could easily take over my life and I couldn't go there. I told myself, "It would all work out."

I knew Mona had to be at her daughter's by now, who also lived in Edmonton. I knew that it wouldn't be long before I would be the one taking care of her. At the time I had no idea that this was all happening for a much more important reason. "Everything happens for a reason." My sister, whom I loved, but never got along with, would soon break my heart completely!

As the phone rang a second time, sure enough, when I looked at the number on the call display, it was her daughter's number that came up. I held my breath and answered. I said "hello," and I heard my sister's voice say "hello" with a half laugh. It was Mona on the other end and although she was pretending to be in a jolly mood, I knew only too well it was an act. She now thought it was funny to show up and surprise me. She had hinted a couple of times about moving in with me and I said "I was happy on my own." It was a hard concept for my sister to understand, but I was clear. My father had already told me that Mona had moved to Edmonton, so I knew she wasn't here just here for a visit. A visit I could handle. "I will come see you tomorrow," she said. "I'll be home," I replied. I know she had to feel my coolness but that wouldn't stop her.

It would cause me to have anxiety listening to Mona go on and on about everyone else's problems, while she refused to ever take care of herself or admit she ever had a problem. My sister liked to paint a picture that her family was all saints, when the rest of our family and friends knew they were only human and made mistakes just like the rest of us. And that was where we clashed.

"Now what?" I asked myself. I could handle having her for a week, but long term? No way! Living alone for so many years I have become a very light sleeper and "sleep" was the medicine for helping my fibromyalgia. Mona had a constant, deep, loud, hacking cough that went on day and night. Sometimes she sounded like she was choking, the cough was so bad. It would seem ten times louder in my small apartment. Lack of sleep would mean more pain for me. Not happening!

Get along or not, we were sisters. Caring for others was my sister's greatest attribute and in the end her biggest downfall, because she never balanced it to take care of herself. Being sisters meant, taking care of one another, which was a code we all lived by. I would take care of her in my own way and still hopefully keep my own sanity.

The next day Mona came knocking on my door with one suitcase and an overnight bag. I could feel my insides shaking as I hugged her. "Be compassionate," I reminded myself. I didn't want to hurt her feelings. I buckled in and practiced what I had learned about meditation and staying positive. I went on walks every day to take a break from her constant talking about how horrible her life was. It could bring the Dalai Lama down to never having any hope in a minute flat. And yes, now she was living with me. What could I do? Mona knew I wouldn't turn her away and I told her after we discussed everything, she could stay with me until we found her a place of her own. I would try and get her a place close by. I knew she wanted to live with me. This would be a challenge.

I believe everyone goes through hard times and needs time to vent, but this negative way of thinking was Mona's downfall. I talked to her about it many times and explained how this constant "my life sucks," attitude was bringing even more bad things to her. She would always say she understood, but did nothing to change it. It was a waste of time talking to her about it, but I didn't give up. I prayed for her always, that a light bulb would go off one day and she would start seeing and living a more positive life.

This was a tricky situation I was now in. Even I couldn't see any humor in being put on the spot like this. This was also the attitude of some people with addictions. Many believe everybody owes them. I was learning daily to be stronger and had lots of practice speaking my mind for many years now but it was still especially hard for me to stand up to my family, especially with someone with a bad temper. I cannot stand arguing and fighting with anyone. Some things were just not worth the battles. I knew I had to leave this one up to God. Miracles do happen every day and this would take a small miracle. I put my trust in Him and I believed I would keep my sanity and it would all work out.

Mona would be speechless sometimes when I refused to overlook her criticism and judgments of me anymore, or I would sometimes ask her the hard questions that I might otherwise be afraid to. She didn't like this new side of me at all. Most people I knew gained a new respect for me when I started standing up for myself and more importantly, I started respecting myself. It took a lot of courage for me to speak my mind.

After almost a month with my depressed, pissed off sister living with me, I managed to get her a unit in the same apartment building I live in. We were both happy with that and we had to come up with the money. I would help her with it as much as I could to get her started. I did talk her into finally seeing a counselor which I believed would be very beneficial to her. I was counseled out by then. Someone outside the family might get through to her. In that month I had listened daily to the same complaints and by then I had given up on giving any advice. I know being a good listener was important and something she needed as well, but I was done. My sister had never taken advice from anyone in her life who tried to help her. I was happy she at least caved on the counselor that might help her deal with the loss of her marriage. It took months but she finally found a lady she liked and went several times to talk to her. I believe it did help her but I feel she needed to go longer to find any real peace in her life. Most importantly, she had to want it.

I looked forward to having my own space back and she was happy to stay close to me. So it was a win-win situation for both of us. For those weeks she stayed with me, I had watched her every day all day long sit, drink coffee and chain smoke with the cigarettes that I was now buying her. She had no money whatsoever when she showed up at my door. My credit card was being used to keep up. I tried not to worry and to keep the faith. I knew Mona's gambling addiction was bad as she had gotten a total of $100,000 in payouts in the year after her break-up with her husband, plus the monthly alimony of $800. For someone like me who had survived quite well on $25 to $35,000 a year for the past fifteen years, getting no alimony from my divorce, that kind of money was mind blowing to me.

Here I was now buying her cigarettes and feeding her?! I would do just about anything for anyone, but this seemed ridiculous in my mind. I tried to be understanding of my family and the addictions but some days I had my limits. Most of the money my sister had received in that past year before her move to Edmonton had gone to gambling. It was sad and I was somewhat hardened to feeling sorry for anyone who did this to themselves. The funny thing was my family couldn't understand why I changed over the years and became tougher. My brother especially said many times. "You've changed," like it was a negative thing. Thankfully I am tougher. If I wasn't, I would surely be in an asylum.

As I write some of these personal stories about my sister and our family, I stop and wonder sometimes what my sister thinks now. My sister that kept everything about herself and her family so tight lipped from those of us that loved her. I tell myself she is fine with it because I told her when we talked about me writing this book I would be honest. She trusted me enough to know I would tell the truth and still be compassionate. That is why I am leaving some things alone.

Mona clearly had a very sweet side and she was well loved by many. She certainly had a gift of caring and was faithful. Deep down she was a good human being and had a good heart. Yes, she had issues, like most of us. Some can be more serious and disruptive in our lives and that's when we may need to seek outside help. I always say, "If we were all alike, it would be a boring world." I believe where my sister is now, she would have a different perspective about being more open and honest about her issues. There is no shame in being human and imperfect.... we all are. Accepting this about ourselves gives us room to make changes and grow. Living in denial is not healthy for anyone. I believe Mona would be happy if we can help a few people who connect with us and may need help in some way. My sister had at least agreed to see a counselor. That was huge and I felt proud of her for making the effort.

I know I maybe should have been more compassionate about Mona losing all her money and showing up at my door, knowing it is a disease, but I wasn't at that moment. She had wasted tens of thousands of dollars gambling and now I was put on the spot. She was also taken advantage of later on when she got her final pay out from her ex. It was a vicious cycle of addiction and I was right in the middle of it all.

The human side of me was angry and frustrated about it because now it was in my lap and I know how it works. I didn't want to be the enabler, again, and I certainly was exhausted from just trying to keep up and take care of myself most days. My number one mission when Mona showed up at my door was to help her get her own place for my sake and then get her into counseling for hers. We did both and we were both happy about it.

Chapter Twenty-One
Family Reunion

I have realized over the years that when people share the same birth sign it makes a huge difference in how they connect and get along in families and amongst friends. I have found that the people with the strongest bonds are usually of the same birth sign. Donna and I were both Libras and we shared many of the same traits and similarities; it was easy for us to get along. Mona and Dad were both Scorpio and they were close. My mother and brother shared the same sign which was Aries and they were close. Maye is a Cancer sign and it makes sense to me now why she may have often felt left out sometimes. Even with all our differences, we all shared three things that bonded us all. We shared the same humor, love of music and love for each other and our family. Those were the bonds that kept us wanting to live close to each other for most of our lives. As we got into our later years and after I went through my divorce, the dynamics changed for us as a family. I was single and liked to socialize as much as was allowed, plus I worked full time and was now a single mom. My sisters and I didn't spend nearly as much time together anymore as we had previously.

When I moved to St. Albert in 2003 and then to Edmonton in 2004, I was already used to not seeing my sisters quite as much as I did in the past. It felt strange for me for quite a while, and I missed them a lot. We kept in touch over the phone and we visited back and forth as much as possible. I got used to being completely alone and having my own routine.

When Mona moved to Edmonton to be with me I hoped she would join me in my walks and doing other activities. I still try and go for walks at least five days a week and I do yoga twice a week. There were only two times in the two years she lived here that she went with me for a walk. "Please try and be active," I would beg her. I would ask her to go swimming, anything to get her out and enjoy life a little. My enjoyments were not my sister's and I had to accept that about us.

Mona was trying to cut back on smoking because I was buying cigarettes for her. She was aware that I couldn't afford it and was down to one pack a day. That was a good thing. I would beg her to cut back because her constant cough was so scary as well. "Okay, I will." she would say. I know our family drove her crazy sometimes with the constant nagging about her chain smoking. Anytime I talked with her about it I could see she would get mad with me. When I would tell her it was because I loved her and worried about her health she would relax and say, "I know." At least she had cut back to a pack a day after staying with me for the first week but that only lasted until she got her own place. Cutting her off completely would be cruel and not good for either of us. She was already going through enough at the time.

Eventually I stopped inviting her to do things with me and I would just go on my own. I didn't like constantly putting her on the spot and there are only so many times someone can say no to someone before they stop asking. Here I was living in Edmonton with no friends to go out and do things with. This should have been a wonderful thing for anyone to have a sister move close to them. I was independent for so long now that I loved it most days but I always tried to include her in my activities and asked many times if there was something she would like to do and I could join her. She would think for a minute and say, "no, not really." It was a whole new life for my sister and I knew it was hard for her to adjust but sometimes it was hard for me to see her like this, especially when she made no effort. She was stuck in the negativity. I finally had to try and focus on keeping myself healthy and let her do what she wanted.

I knew Mona was depressed and I consoled her as much as I possibly could but I also knew she was partly responsible for the mess she was in right now, and no one else. That was hard to swallow when I was in therapy myself many years before and a real eye opener for me. I was responsible for myself and the situations I put myself in. I tried to help her understand this about herself many times so she wouldn't be so angry with others, but it seemed hopeless to get her to be responsible in any way. My sister was so angry for so many years she didn't know how to be any other way.

My spirit had been completely broken and I worked hard for many years to heal myself. There is no better reward than finally loving the person you see in the mirror. My sister was broken too, only in a different way and I wanted nothing more for her than to love that person she saw in the mirror every day. To get her to open up was never an easy task. We have to be honest with ourselves before we can be honest with others. The best lesson I have taught my children in life is to admit and accept when there's a problem, be real, and ask for outside help whenever it's needed.

Mona was also suffering and depressed because after being with one man for 40 years and although they split up, she still loved him. The break up was not her choice. It was a big adjustment for her, even though she had moved out of her home in

Fort McMurray and shared a place with our brother for a while; she was still stuck in the past. I told her I would do everything I could to help her and I tried my very best to encourage her to make positive changes for herself. She would do things as slow or fast as she wanted and I had to respect it. It was all her choices now, even if it wasn't healthy and I didn't agree, I had to back off.

Our brother moved to Edmonton a few months after Mona arrived at my door and he wanted to move in with her. She told him he had to get his own place so she was at least putting her own foot down for once with him. This was good. They were not getting along before she left Fort McMurray. They were both deep into their addictions while they lived together. He became drug free when he first moved here, which was great. He eventually ended up moving into his own place in my apartment block as well. His attitude about life was even more negative than my sister. I struggled to be around it. I hoped he would at least stay clean from crack. The owners of my apartment block were understanding and gave him a chance to rent here.

I am probably the softest person on earth who has had to toughen up to survive. I may come across as harsh sometimes but I had learned a lot from my past mistakes and I had learned the hard way, when to say "no." I am sure it was a shock to my family when I started saying no to them sometimes. My brother knew better than to even ask to live with me. I had turned my own son down and my brother knew, I knew, he had been using drugs again. I had always been a people pleaser and my needs came last for many years but with counseling, wisdom and growth, I knew taking care of number one was of the utmost importance to be able to care for anyone else.

The building we all now lived in is a quiet, clean building and the rent is reasonable. Junior was renting a two bedroom apartment, two floors below me and he eventually moved his girlfriend in with him.

Now, as I sit here and write about it all, some of it seems humorous to me. There's not much in this life that I can't find humor in. I could almost see my family in a sitcom sometimes, especially with all three of us living in the same apartment block. I never dreamed in a million years that this would happen when I moved here.

Mona's apartment was a cozy one bedroom just one floor down from mine. My parking space was right in front of her patio window. Suddenly after answering to no one for fifteen years, I couldn't go anywhere without my sister poking her head out the patio window and asking me where I was going. If I was gone for more than an hour or two she was watching for me to come home. She had been worried about me... "Please don't worry," I would tell her. Now, I felt my freedom to come and go without answering to anyone was gone. As annoying as it was back then, now the memory warms my heart. My three children and my grandchildren were all living here at the time and I tried to spend time with them as often as possible. Little did I know that I would soon wish for my sister to be there checking up on me.

On occasions I would still ask my sister to go out with me, to see a movie or dinner, anything to try and help her get out of her apartment. It could have been great for both of us but the answer was always the same. I would visit her just about every day or she would come to my place. We did love to watch our favorite shows together and I enjoyed those times.

When Mona's friend Theresa came to visit from Fort McMurray and stayed with her family here in Edmonton, she would invite Mona to dinner or a movie, and Mona would go with her, every time. It spoke volumes about our relationship.

Chapter Twenty-Two

The First Signs

Nearly one year after Mona moved down stairs from me, in August of 2012, she started calling me up almost daily, complaining of having a lot of pain in her right shoulder and back area. She had a chest x-ray taken in July because of her emphysema and she was told everything was good. She had no pain in that area at that time but had some neck pain which is normal for fibromyalgia patients. This pain in her back came on very suddenly. I would go downstairs with her and gently rub her back trying to help take some of the pain away. She had gone to the doctors quite often over the past ten years for tests and had found out she had fibromyalgia. She was used to body pain as a rule, but she said, "This feels different." She went to our family doctor and he ran a couple of tests. She had lost her appetite because she felt stomach sick all the time. The first set of tests came back showing her esophagus was not working properly and she had medicine that was supposed to help her with it. The medicine only helped a little and for a very short period of time.

By the middle of October, I would go downstairs to her apartment and rub her back for her daily. She was now throwing up this foamy substance on occasion and I was getting worried. I urged her to go back to the doctor and she did. He gave her a prescription for pain medication and he was sending her to see a specialist. She had no choice but to take the meds now because the pain was so bad. My sister couldn't stand to swallow an aspirin. One night when she was having intense pain I took her to the emergency department at the hospital. The doctor there took another x-ray of her chest and did several other tests. I went to get her a drink and I saw chest x-rays posted up on a screen in the hallway on the ward we were at. I wondered if it was my sisters and I remember seeing a strange looking cloudy spot on that x-ray. To this day I don't know for sure if it was Mona's but I am willing to bet that it was. The doctor sent her home and said nothing to her about it that night but two days later he called her. He told her something showed up on the x-ray and she needed to go see her family doctor for more tests. She called me at home and I could hear the worry in her voice. We went back to see our doctor and he made an appointment for her to see an oncologist to have further tests done. He assured her that in his opinion, it was a cyst, nothing to worry about. That eased her mind and I chose to believe our family doctors opinion for now.

Mona went to several appointments around this time including the oncologist. They did all the testing, including a biopsy. By now she had started throwing up more often and at times, she said "there is blood in it." I was getting more concerned, even though the family doctor said he was not worried. I was going down to her place to stay with her most afternoons and evenings or if she felt up to it she would climb the two flights of stairs to my place. The worst part was no matter how much pain medication she was taking, she still had pain. We would watch our favorite shows together, especially at the beginning of the week when Dancing With the Stars, American Idol, Nashville and Family Feud came on. Junior and his girlfriend would come to Mona's to visit and sometimes do her laundry for her when she started to struggle going up and down the stairs. We all picked up her groceries and I helped by cleaning her place when needed.

Quite often Junior and his girlfriend went with Mona to her doctor's appointments and they were the ones who took her for her first biopsy. Junior was doing well at staying clean at that time and he was a big help in those first months. Junior and I went with Mona in late October for the test results from the biopsy of her lung. Junior went for a walk while Mona and I sat in the little office with a window overlooking downtown Edmonton. I was nervous but trying to stay positive and repeating the usual mantras inside my head, "everything will be fine." I felt very sorry for my sister; I knew she had to be worried sick. She hid it well.

Finally the slender, young, pretty doctor walked in the tiny room. She sat across from us on a stool and started telling Mona the results of the first biopsy. When she said "they found no cancer," Mona jumped off the stool she was sitting on and hugged the doctor. The doctor went on to say, "This is not one hundred percent you realize. Nothing showed up but we are going to keep an eye on it." It was a big relief for me and Mona was ecstatic! She was still in a lot of pain and was taking the prescribed pain medication on a regular basis. She was now taking morphine in a pill form. She found she was getting stomach sick from them, so she starting taking a pill for nausea as well. When the morphine wasn't working, it was changed to oxycodone. Having been through this with Donna with the pain pills, it concerned me and I expressed it to Mona she had to be careful and ask for something less addictive. From what we found out, they were all addictive, she had no choice but to take them or suffer more. Taking them now and then may be okay but she was taking a lot for a long period of time by now.

This was ongoing up until the end of November into December when things started to take a change for the worse. Over the next two months she had her main pills every four hours and her break through pills when needed, which was every two hours. They were a lower dose of her main pain pills of whatever she was prescribed at the time. Eventually it started to poison her system. We as a family had no idea what was going on, we were doing what we were told by the doctors. We would soon learn a lot more about what pain medication can do to our bodies and minds.

Chapter Twenty-Three

Heartbreaking News

Two weeks before Christmas Mona's oldest son Kenny and his girlfriend came to Edmonton from Fort McMurray to spend Christmas with her. He had been laid off from work, so the timing was good for them. I was relieved because taking care of her was taking a toll on me, even with other family helping. It would give me peace of mind knowing he was with her at night. I was also happy to have my oldest nephew around because I was close to him and we got along well. He was like a son to me.

By that time Mona was having severe pain and it seemed like the pain meds were not doing a thing to help her. We took turns rubbing the constant pain in her back and she was losing weight. Mona would stand and lean on the table or counter top, crying and moaning in agony. I felt helpless! It seemed no matter what the doctor prescribed it would only give her brief relief and then the pain would come back stronger before her next dosage of meds. It was very hard to watch my sister suffer this way. I was becoming more worried than I wanted to be. Her son and I would look at each other and just shake our heads feeling helpless.

I was looking forward to having all the family together for Christmas because we hadn't had this many family members together for many years although Junior started staying away for weeks at a time and that would upset Mona and in turn, upset me. I had become Mona's protector by now.

We weren't sure if Junior was using drugs again or not, but Mona and I had a strong hunch he was. He finally admitted to me long after her death that he had been. No matter how many times we asked him if he was using, he would lie. At least if he had told the truth, Mona would have understood better why he wouldn't come to see her. I can live with truth and she wouldn't have felt like he didn't care. Nothing angers me more than lying. Many addicts lie but it doesn't make it okay. If he would have said, "I'm sorry I am using and not capable of being there." Not a problem, I could accept that. This behavior continued over the next six months with Junior. The excuses were never ending. I had to let it go and focus on my sister.

Christmas day Junior did participate with the meal. We were very happy to have everyone together. This was extra special to me having spent some Christmases alone after leaving Fort McMurray. We all shared in the cooking of Christmas dinner. We had a set time when we would meet and eat, so when the food I made was ready I took it down to my sisters. Everyone was there in her apartment already, sitting wherever there was space. The sad part was my sister could hardly eat a bite. I took her a plate of food and sat next to her on the sofa. When I passed her the plate she said "I will try," but she only ate two small bites and that was all. She was constantly rocking her body from the pain. Her eyes closed, face tightened from the agony. When I had first walked in and saw her sitting in the corner of the couch with her blanket around her, slowly rocking and quietly weeping, I was disturbed that nobody else was paying any attention to her. Seeing her like this was now normal for us. It was pitiful to watch!

This would all eventually have an effect on my own health. I was feeling heaviness and tightness in my entire body that was causing more pain for me. I wasn't sleeping well and that didn't help. It was overwhelming sitting there watching her suffer and unable to do anything but get things for her and rub her back. The anxiety was building and I was doing everything I could to relieve some of it. I would even walk the hallways in my apartment block to get some exercise in and try and release some of the stress.

Just after Christmas, Kenny went to Sylvan Lake to pick up his two daughters who had just got back from a trip to Mexico with their mom and step dad. I went down to see them that evening after they arrived and we all gathered to watch them open their Christmas presents. They are beautiful girls who loved their grandma. They had a great time opening their gifts and Mona tried to enjoy it as much as she could. I could see her agony written all over her face. Mona was an outstanding, wonderful grandmother and her grandchildren loved her dearly. This was where her sweet side came out whenever they were around her. There was nothing she wouldn't do for any of them.

The pain medicine was doing nothing to help her by now. She wasn't getting any amount of relief like she was weeks before. No matter how many times we went to the doctors at the emergency or our family doctor, the pain pill dosage was increased. Our family doctor told us at one point that the pain medicine she was taking was a lot, and it should have been helping. All the tests had been done. We just hoped and prayed that the cyst she had on her lung would heal and give her some kind of relief soon. She had been suffering daily for over four months and it was only getting worse every day. The bottles of unused pain meds were stacking up in her cupboard because the dosage or type of drug would change from one week to the next. Her son was great for running around and taking care of her medications and groceries now that he was here. It was a tremendous help.

One of Mona's grandkids had been sick when she came home from Mexico. Nobody seemed to be concerned about it, but I was. It was the next evening when I was at my place when her daughter came upstairs to tell me "Mom might have caught the flu bug. She suddenly has a fever." Sure enough Mona ended up in emergency that night. She was quarantined right away because somebody had mentioned to the staff the sick grandchild had been to Mexico. No fault of her granddaughter at all, and in the end, it turned out to be a good thing. We would finally get some answers of why my sister was in so much pain.

Mona was in the hospital for a week this time. She was taken to a private room and kept under quarantine until all the tests were finished. After three days, they finally found out that the flu bug she had was usually found in birds. They treated her right away with antibiotics. In the meantime the doctors, including her oncologist decided to do another biopsy on her lung. I was there every day with her and on the sixth day, I said to her "I have to stay home tomorrow and get some things done," and she said, "yes, do that." Junior and his girlfriend were there at the time and said they would make sure they went the next day so she wouldn't be alone. My brother was coming around again and that made us happy. We were all hoping she would get out in the next couple of days once all the reports were back.

The next afternoon I was home doing my laundry when the phone rang, I answered and to my surprise it was Mona's oncologist, Dr. Smith. I was very surprised she had called me. I braced myself for what was coming. "Are you going to be seeing Mona today?" she asked.

"No I won't, I had to get some things done at home today. I had been there every day with her but my brother is there today." I replied. I asked hesitantly, "Is everything okay?"

She said, "Yes, I was just wondering how you were all coping and if you have any questions anytime, just call me."

I said, "Okay, I will, thank you," I hung up a little puzzled by the call. "Well, that was nice of her," I thought. But my instinct was telling me something was up.

There had been another oncologist taking care of my sister as well. He was Dr. Smith's assistant. He was usually there to see Mona early in the mornings.

Later that afternoon Junior called me and said, the doctors were releasing Mona and he was bringing her home. I was very happy to hear that and I asked him to call me as soon as they arrived. It was two hours later when I received the call that they were home. I went downstairs to my sister's apartment. Junior, his girlfriend, Mona and her daughter were all there. I gave Mona a hug and chatted briefly talking about the day. I told her how I had got a call from her doctor which seemed strange. Her granddaughters had already left and gone back to Sylvan Lake. Kenny was not there at that moment either.

My sister had two couches set up in her living room. She was sitting on one couch, Junior was standing up behind it and his girlfriend was sitting next to Mona. I was on the other couch and Mona's daughter was sitting next to me. Junior's girlfriend suddenly got up and came and sat between myself and Mona's daughter. She caught hold of my hand and wrapped her arm around my shoulder tight. I thought to myself, "What the heck is going on?" I just looked at them all, looking at me and Junior spoke up and asked Mona, "Do you want to tell her or should I?" I thought, "Uh oh, here it comes!"

Mona spoke up and said, "I have cancer." Junior went on to say, "she has six months to a year to live without treatments, one year to eighteen months with treatments." He made a gesture of flinging his hands from his side to up into the air. The treatments would be radiation. When it sunk in what they were saying, my hands automatically went up to cover my face, and I cried, "NOT AGAIN! NO, NOT AGAIN!" This could not be happening again! How is this even possible?! This was beyond upsetting as I tried to take in what they had said. She was going to die too??!! My poor sister!! My God, my heart!!

Now it was clear why her doctor had called me, she wanted to know if I was going to the hospital before they told Mona, she would never tell me this news over the phone. I felt sick and my mind was racing, worried about Mona and yes, selfishly worried about myself. I had close to a nervous breakdown once before, I couldn't ever let it happen again. How would I survive this?! I was also angry at Mona for not trying to cut back on smoking after all of us begging her for so long. Now she was going to die?! My brain kept racing! I could feel the tension in my body and the pain right away in my lower back. "Calm down and breathe," I told myself, realizing how my reaction was affecting my own body and mind already. "Accept it, deal with it" a voice whispered. My sister had to have been feeling a million different emotions! There were no words exchanged at that moment, I couldn't even look at her! I just cried!

Kenny came home shortly after they broke the news to me. I pulled myself together and we sat around and tried to act normal as I waited for someone to tell him. Everybody was sitting around the living room for about ten minutes and nobody was saying a word other than the little bit of banter going on between him and his mom. I sat there thinking "someone needs to tell him," as I fought off the tears. Kenny was lecturing his mom a little because she had come home with an oxygen tank she now had to use, and that upset him. I didn't think it was my place to tell him and that made me mad. Finally I looked at him sitting on the floor across from me and I said to him in the gentlest voice I could speak, "this is not good son." He looked at me and asked "No?"

I said, "No, your mom has cancer."

He got up and went to the bathroom and threw up. That was his usual reaction to stress. My heart broke for him and the rest of her children. When he came back out, Junior filled him in on the rest of the details. He was devastated, as were all her children. They may have been products of a dysfunctional home, just like my kids had been, and each had their own set of issues with their mother, but one thing I knew for sure, they loved her.

Mona's reaction was no tears, just deep anger and sarcasm. She was making jokes packed with venom. She was undoubtedly angry. The type of cancer she had was most likely caused from smoking. I would imagine she was mad at herself more than anyone else, but I doubted it. That was my sister's attitude towards life in general, that everything bad would come her way, and it did, but it was never her fault. I can't imagine the emotions she was feeling, I just knew my own, and I was devastated and truth be told, a little pissed at her too. She had been diagnosed with "Stage 4, squamous cell carcinoma." It was found in the area behind her esophagus and in her lung. It had spread towards her spinal area. We found out later it was in her forth rib. That explained the area of all her torturous pain.

Kenny came out of the bathroom, went behind his mother wrapped his arms around her neck and sobbed. I was frozen to the seat. I didn't know what to do. I felt like jumping up and running away from it all. That's what I really wanted to do, but I knew I would have to face this head on as well.

Mona always seemed to want to carry the family's burdens and dwell on them without seeming to care how critical it was to her own health. She was definitely the martyr in our family. Taking care of everyone, covering up for everyone and carrying all her own secrets definitely caused my sister to overindulge in cigarettes, coffee and gambling. She had all the warning signs from the chain smoking for years. Mona had the deep hacking cough since she was thirty years old and the emphysema she was diagnosed with ten years before but it wasn't enough to make her even cut back. With all the worrying she did over the years about the whole family and trying to control it all, she never once considered how something like this would affect us all. It had to eventually catch up to her and here we all were, right in the center of it. There was no getting out for me, I knew that. It is sad to think of how that much pressure my oldest sister put on herself. We all have our roles in families and this had been Mona's all her life and she had loved it. Now she had no control left at all, over this or anything else. It must have been frightening for her. I knew the anger she showed now was coming from pure fear. Yes, I was angry too. I tried my best to not show her I was. I knew she had to feel awful enough. She had many issues; however, I would never take away from her devotion to family. Now we all had to be there for her 100%! At least I knew I would be.

    You would never say Mona had a problem if you asked her. Our whole lives she pretended her life was perfect. I realized one day a few years before she died that her whole immediate family had been on medication for stress, except her. That says a lot about the dynamics in her home.

Chapter Twenty-Four
Middle of the Night

I was thinking about going back to work after Christmas of 2012. My unemployment was running out. I certainly was not feeling well enough to go back to work but I felt I had no choice. I saw what Mona went through applying for disability with her fibromyalgia, and she had a lot of doctor's reports to back her up. I did not. I had just lived with the pain over the years. For many years I thought it was arthritis, but now I knew what it was and the pain was getting worse every year I remained working. I was going to put a few resumes out after Christmas and hopefully find something part time.

It had been two weeks after Christmas when Mona was told she had cancer and it was terminal. Now, what would I do?! Even though her son had said he would stay with her, I knew it was too much for one person, just watching her in constant agony for the past four months was exhausting for me or anyone around her. I also had the added stress of needing to go back to work. We all needed support.

My ex-boyfriend Barry contacted me around this time. He stayed in touch more often checking in on Mona. He wanted me to take the time I needed to help take care of Mona and he offered to pay my monthly bills. I struggled with that because I am so independent. I knew and he knew I couldn't mentally or physically do both. The offer was very kind. To let someone else take care of me for a while would be nice. I would have to give in and let go of my pride which is not easy for me. I was scared because my life had been controlled for so many years by someone else paying the bills, and being independent for so long was a feeling I liked. Even though Barry was a good guy and would do whatever I needed, I worried about his gambling addiction and with him following through, but I decided to take the risk for my sake and my sisters and am glad I did. Barry was working and living in Fort McMurray at the time and said he could afford it. He said, "You helped me before, now it's my time to help you." I took the risk and he followed through. Barry helped pay my bills for the next thirteen months. I am forever grateful and thank him for that. It was a big deal and allowed me to spend that time helping my sister and healing myself! I did go back to work part-time the following Christmas.

 Five to six weeks after Mona was diagnosed with cancer she began to have a lot of swelling in her feet and legs. She was starting to forget things and became sort of lost sometimes. It was really hard because she wasn't sleeping at night. She would have her naps during the day and up all night. Sometimes she didn't even seem to know what she was doing. The doctor's appointments were not helping solve this issue and it would take some time before it would be solved.

 In the meantime, Kenny would take breaks and occasionally go out with his friends on the weekend or go to Fort McMurray for a few days. He needed the breaks and I was glad he took them but I struggled to take care of her alone when she was up all night long. This was a very difficult time. My kids were all working and my brother was nowhere to be seen again. If I didn't have fibromyalgia, I could have cared less if I got much sleep. I did my best not to complain about my own health issues and sucked it up. My sister had a death sentence. There was nothing worse!

One night I was sleeping at home in my lazy boy and I suddenly heard Mona cough. I would recognize her cough anywhere, even if she were a mile away. Because my apartment was so stuffy and even though it was cold outside, I kept my spare room window opened just a crack some nights. Hearing her cough was nothing strange to me because I had heard it often when she would be outside on her patio smoking. She wasn't smoking at this time, because she was finally wearing a patch. "I guess she's getting some air." I thought. Her son was with her and I wasn't concerned. It was already four in the morning and I was still trying to get some sleep, so I closed my eyes and thought nothing more of it until my buzzer rang in my apartment. I sat straight up in my chair thinking "who in the world is buzzing me this time of the morning?" This was about twenty minutes after I had heard her cough. I got up, pressed the button and said "Hello." This voice came back saying, "Diane, can you let me in?"

I froze right away and my heart started racing. It was Mona! I pushed the buzzer to let her in and forced myself to race in my bedroom to grab my housecoat. I thought, "What in the heck is she doing outside at four in the morning?" I pulled on some sandals, forgot to grab my glasses and rushed down the stairs, as fast as my body would let me. I rushed to the front entrance of the building. There was no sign of her. My heart was beating out of my chest, "Oh my God," I thought, "She can't be outside." It was -20 degrees!! I rushed back up one flight of stairs to her apartment and the door was locked. I knocked lightly at first, because I didn't want to stir the neighbors but then I started to panic and knocked harder, not caring who I woke up at this point, it was then I heard movement at the end of the hallway. I turned my head to look and focused at the figure standing there and Mona was just at the top of the stairs that led up from the basement. I said, "Sister, what are you doing??"

"I don't know," she replied sounding exhausted. She sat down on the bottom step from the upper floor and put her head in her hands. When I got closer to her, because I didn't have my glasses on, I couldn't really see clearly what she was wearing. I heard the caretaker's voice call from upstairs, "Diane, is she alright?" I said "She went outside and her door is locked, can you let us in her apartment please?" He and his wife were awake because apparently Mona had buzzed them before she buzzed me. He said, "Hang on, I will get the keys." When she stood up, I saw she was wearing her slippers, grey jogging pants, her son's coat that was too small so she couldn't close it. It was at that moment that I realized my sister's top half was naked under the opened coat. She was out of it, not aware of what she was doing. My heart dropped when I saw this because I knew she would be devastated to know anyone would see her like this, never mind she could have frozen to death.

Just then the caretaker came down and walked in front of us to unlock her apartment door. I took Monas hand and lead her down the hallway behind him. I held the coat together for her and took her inside. Kenny was sound asleep on the couch. I sent Mona in the room to put a shirt on and I woke him up. She was like a lost soul. It is heartbreaking to remember. Even today that memory still upsets me and makes me cry.

Her son was shocked when I woke him up. He had been in a deep sleep. It was very hard on everyone at this point trying to keep up with taking care of my sister in this state. We both looked at each other and started to cry when I told him what happened, trying our best for her not to see us. I told her when she came out of the bedroom, "You can't go outside in the middle of the night."

She never realized fully what she had done. "I know," she said and she kept repeating that she fell and hurt her back. I checked her back and saw no signs of anything. In those moments I believe she would forget she had cancer. She was confused about the pain in her back. When she was more alert the next day, Kenny told her a little of what happened and it scared her. He didn't tell her how she had been dressed. To think of what could have happened to her when she was out there wandering around alone and confused at 4 a.m. was too much for me to imagine. I regretted not getting up and checking when I first heard her cough because I am certain she was outside in the parking lot then, not on her patio as I thought. Thankfully she was lucid enough to come back inside and buzz my apartment. We believed she was trying to go to the store to buy cigarettes because this was first when she was wearing the patch the doctor gave her to try and quit smoking. After that night, Kenny placed spoons and butter knives all along the front door frame, so that if she tried to get out again, he would hear her.

  The next day when I went down to her apartment we decided we had to take her back to the hospital. She got very angry and upset whenever we talked of taking her there. Mona begged us not to take her and we promised we wouldn't, only if we had to. There was no doubt she was very afraid that it might be her last time and she wouldn't come home. Little did we know at the time but it was actually giving her more time by taking her back there that day. It took a couple of days to talk her into it. Her son was on the phone calling her doctor and they said to bring her in. By this time she was having trouble communicating and she was sleeping a lot during the day. The doctors were prescribing stronger medication and telling us to give her the breakthrough pills whenever she needed them, which by this point was every hour or two. She would take two extra little pills. By now she was taking up to forty pills a day, including her other meds for nausea and blood pressure. Finally after much persistence, we talked her into going. We got her in the car and were on the way to the cancer hospital. Mona had been barely eating anything and her legs and feet were swollen out of shape. She was going around in circles, completely confused sometimes.

The doctors assessed her in a hospital room. They had her on a bed asking her simple questions like, "Where are you now? What year is it?" She was having trouble answering them. Then it came to a point where she wasn't responding at all. I started to quietly weep watching her and so did her son. The one doctor took my nephew outside and talked to him and when they came back in, they had decided to keep her in. We were told her condition was caused from too much calcium build up in her blood. From what we understood, we thought it was from the cancer that had spread into her bones that caused it. We should have asked more questions. Nobody had told us any different or spoke of what caused it. The doctor said they could give her a drip to clear it up and it would help with the confusion and swelling she was having.

Mona was placed on a ward for the very sick patients. She had a room to herself and we would go see her every day. The first time I went into this hospital with her, it was like deja vu all over again for me because I had been there when Donna had cancer. I felt a lot of anxiety going in there then, and now with Mona. We were on the floor where the patients were staying. I saw the very sick, some walking around and some in their beds. Many were critical. My heart was breaking for each and every one of them. Some had visitors, some were alone. I could only imagine the loneliness. It felt like hell to me to me at first glance, a place where people only suffered but then I also saw and felt the love and care there from the doctors and nurses.

The nurses were wonderful and day by day, Mona was getting a little more alert with each treatment. By day three we went for a walk downstairs and looked around the gift shop. I was happy to see her getting back to herself and she would soon be going home. I bought her a beautiful sky blue and white crocheted blanket from the gift shop that she loved. When I wrapped it around her shoulders, she closed her eyes and smiled at the feel of it. "Ooohhhh, I want to be buried in this." she said. A statement like that was rare from her and stunned me because she seemed in denial about her prognosis most days. Normally she was very afraid and didn't want to talk about it at all. Most of her remarks when she was more alert were in anger.

This time Mona was in the hospital for a week and not once did anyone mention to us that she was being poisoned from all the pain medications she was on. I would find this out a month later. The pain specialist made a few changes to her meds when we took her home but it was still a lot. The swelling had gone down some and she was definitely more awake and alert, but not fully. I was happy she was at least feeling better and eating a little more. She had also decided to take the radiation treatments, or at least try them.

Chapter Twenty-Five

Criminal Acts

Even with all the heartache of my sister suffering, there were many lighthearted moments as well. There is no better time to find humor and laughter as it is when you are under stress. It brings much needed relief! Mona was having so much trouble eating and she continued to lose weight. She had lost 40 pounds by now and would lose more over the next couple of months. She also suffered with major heartburn. I started cutting up apples for her to help with the heartburn, and it did help. A piece of apple and a drink of water do wonders for my heartburn. Something I had learned after having my gall bladder removed years before. I was having terrible heartburn and a doctor prescribed meds for it, I asked if there was a home remedy for heartburn he could suggest, he said "No." I went home and looked up "home remedies for heartburn," on my computer and found out a piece of apple and water after eating did the trick! I have used it ever since. It helped my sister as well.

    Mona went from eating grapes for a while to watermelon. It would change all the time what she liked and managed to eat. She seemed to tolerate fruit the most, but it was always very small portions. There were days when she would smell things burning when we couldn't. We read and heard different reasons as to why that was happening. One was the meds she was taking affected her sense of smell. She had to have her water glass filled constantly with ice in order to sip a little bit of water. Some days she barely drank four ounces when she was taking the radiation treatments.

I had already asked a couple of doctors about prescribing medical marijuana for her, to help her sleep better and eat. None of them wanted to do it. I still don't understand this?! Our mistake several times was going along with what every doctor said, believing and having faith that they always knew what they all were talking about, and so we should trust them. You have to learn to trust your own instincts as well. None of us as a family ever argued with them. I wish now we would have pushed more for the medical marijuana.

One day when myself, Kenny, my son Jesse and a couple of other family members were at her place, we were all really concerned and discussing how she was hardly eating anything. Each radiation treatment was making it even harder for her to eat and drink. This particular day when we were all together at Sister's apartment, someone mentioned again, the idea of getting her some weed to help her at least eat something and for the first time, she didn't fight us on it. We all mentioned getting it for her before, but she had always said "No." My sister and I were real strict when it came to doing anything to break the law, especially dealing with illegal drugs of any kind. Setting a good example for my kids mattered more to me than anything. But this time, I was in total agreement. I said to one family member that I knew had used it in the past, "I will drive you if you can show me where to go and buy the weed." Breaking the law was the least of my concerns at this point. I wanted to help my sister any way I could and so did the rest of the family.

So, off we went to buy the weed. We had forty dollars. I was a little paranoid when we arrived at the dealer's house and I sat in the "getaway car," waiting impatiently, wondering if I should have disguised myself while picking up my sunglasses and putting them on. Then I became paranoid that putting the glasses on in the middle of winter on a cloudy day, might make me look even more criminal, so I took them off, tossing them back in the holder. I prayed that I wouldn't get arrested for this. I kept telling myself it was for a good cause. For someone that couldn't tell a lie if it killed me, I knew I would confess to the crime right away if a cop pulled up and asked me what I was doing sitting there. Finally my partner in crime came out and got in the car. I could smell the stench of it right away. It always smelled like horse manure to me whenever someone around me was using it in the past. It smelled gross, but it was necessary.

Needless to say, this turned out to be one of our better days with my sister. Everybody was in good humor about the weed and cracking jokes. When we got back a family member sat at the table and rolled up ten joints from our hoist *grinning.* I am pretty sure I am using the old language to describe this contraband. I don't know the new lingo. When he finished, I told Mona I would go out with her on the patio to smoke it. I didn't plan on smoking any but I told her I might, to get her to try it. My son, nephew and others were having quite the chuckle at the prospects of seeing their mothers "stoned." We stepped out on the patio, Mona asked me to light it. "Okay," I said, not really wanting to, but again, anything to help her. There was a little piece of cardboard in one end of the joint. I assumed it was the end I needed to light. I lit it up and passed it to my sister. She was still procrastinating about doing it but finally sucked back three quick puffs and held it. She passed the joint back to me. I didn't take any but would have if I needed to convince her. When she let it out of her lungs, she said, "That's enough," and shook her head with disgust from the taste.

I opened the patio door and we went back inside. I said "what should I do with this?" holding out the joint. They all freaked out and started laughing saying, "Don't bring it in here!!" I was going to flush it, but one of them took it from me and went and flushed it. They were all laughing deliriously when they noticed I had lit the wrong end. "Oh well," I said, "I am not exactly an expert," enjoying the light heartedness of it all.

About five minutes later, my son asked Mona if she wanted to try a chocolate raspberry pie he had brought from a burger chain earlier. Now keep in mind, we couldn't get her to eat or barely drink anything at this point. "Yes," she said, "I will try it." We all looked at each other with a look of accomplishment. This was great!! She took the little pie out of the box, took the first bite and she said "Mmmm." I was amazed she was eating it, much less actually enjoying it. She finished off the whole pie. We were delighted, mission accomplished!!! She had not enjoyed a morsel of food for months and we had tried everything we thought she would like. To actually see her not only eat something, but to enjoy it was worth more than a million dollars to all of us!!

A few minutes later Mona came to sit next to me on the couch. She sat herself down and wrapped both her arms around me, closed her eyes and snuggled into my chest. I wrapped my arm around her and held her there. Someone asked her if she was relaxed. "Yes, I'm too frigging relaxed now," she said with a grin, and we all roared laughing. We sat there like that for a good half an hour with her cuddling into me. It was one of the most fun and most heart filled moments that I had with my sister for quite a while.

That was the one and only time we could convince her to smoke the weed. I think with the standards we set for ourselves as parents, she was not comfortable with the fact that her kids knew she was smoking it, for any reason, and that is sad. It would surely have benefited her in many ways. The rest went in the freezer and eventually I flushed it all. It has been suggested to me that it would help with my fibromyalgia. I have yet to give into it, but if I ever get to the point of really needing it, I will try the medical marijuana.

Chapter Twenty-Six

Dr. Angel

Mona was steadily getting worse with every passing day. She only took four radiation treatments because they were too hard on her system. She was very torn on what to do, mostly because she didn't want to upset her family. We discussed it with her and agreed with her decision that quality of life was more important at this point and I believe she made the right choice for herself. It might have given her a couple more months to live if she had continued with the treatments, but she would have been much sicker getting there. It is a totally different experience and choice for everyone.

Kenny and I sat in the little room with her at the Cancer hospital as she told the doctor she didn't want any more treatments. She was very weak from not eating and hardly drinking anything. The doctor kept looking at me and her son. Both of us had tears rolling down our cheeks as we silently cried. She was stopping the treatments, and I couldn't blame her, but it hurt! The radiation treatments were too hard for her to handle. All I could do now was pray that she didn't suffer even more pain. She was suffering way too much already and it was draining not only her but all of us who loved her. It was going to be a battle for me to accept in my heart but my brain was telling me she shouldn't suffer anymore.

We waited afterwards for the pain specialist because she needed her meds changed AGAIN because the pain wasn't slacking off at all. She had a lot of swelling in her legs and feet again and she was getting to the point where she wasn't sleeping at night again. The pain specialist showed up with her associate and they told us the amount of medication she was taking for pain was too much. We told them exactly what she was taking and the times she took them. She was only taking what was prescribed. This specialist changed her prescription again. Nothing seemed to make that much difference to her pain level. We were at a loss on how to help her. She was still crying in pain in her back and shoulder day after day. She would only get some relief when she was napping right after her main pills, for about twenty minute intervals, sometimes if she was lucky, a little longer. When she got to the point of swelling again, she slept longer until she became hard to get a response from again. Those times were very scary! We took her home that day but I knew in my heart, she wouldn't be there long before she would be back in the hospital. The doctors said they could make a room available for her at "The Grey Nuns Hospital." She wouldn't hear of going in the hospital again.

  Three days later we had to talk to her about going back to the hospital. Her son called me in the morning and asked me to come down, he was burnt out. He was crying and said to me, "She has to go to the hospital Aunt Diane." "Okay, I'll be right there." I replied. I knew it was going to be a battle. I knew I had to be the bad guy but I didn't care. We needed help!

  Junior and his girlfriend came up from their place and we all gently talked to her about going to the hospital again. She was becoming incoherent again. Mona would just start to cry and say she didn't want to go and beg us not to take her. She saw the hospital as her death and she was petrified. Finally after some coaxing and not giving in to her, she agreed to at least go and get checked out. Her son said he didn't want to go and my brother didn't want to so I ended up taking her alone. She was already taking her anger out on me with some of her remarks, this was just another reason for her to hate me and believe me, she did!

I took her to the emergency room at the hospital closer to home. The nurse at the front desk at the hospital was wonderful. I had Mona in a wheelchair with her oxygen tank attached to the back. I told the nurse why I brought my sister in. The nurse whispered to me that her mom had passed of cancer and she was very compassionate towards us. She said because she was a nurse, looking after her mom was left for her to do. She knew how hard it was on a family. "I will get her in quickly." she said. She was a tall, pretty nurse with short blond hair. I took her hand and said, "Thank you." I knew she recognized the tears of worry and exhaustion in my eyes. We understood each other and it gave me some comfort. She was very respectful towards Mona and me. I felt at ease, that someone in the health care system connected with me and my sister. Living in a big city, many times you end up feeling like just another number. The waiting room was full as usual and we did wait for about an hour which was fast at that hospital. Meeting people like that nurse made my day when things were really tough. Nurses are angels in my book.

The doctor we saw ended up admitting Mona and I stayed with her until she was settled. She was making snide remarks to me and glaring at me like I was the devil himself. I thought to myself, "yes, go ahead, take it out on me, I can handle it." I ignored her glares and I kissed her goodnight and said, "I will see you tomorrow," and left. It was torture to leave and torture to stay. I had no choice and the guilt set in again.

I did my very best to not lose my patience with her and tried to always remember, she was scared and drugged. I tried not to take it to heart. However, there were a few days when my empathy was stretched to its limits. This was one of them. The first time they admitted her at the cancer hospital she was not coherent, this time she was. I was definitely the bad guy to her and she let me know it.

It was the end of February by now and the past eighteen months had been an overload of negativity and sickness and it was definitely taking its toll on me. I felt so many mixed emotions watching my sister sometimes. I reassured her I would not leave her when she would ask where this person or that person was when they would stay away. I could see she was hurt. "I won't leave you Sister, I promise." I repeated, feeling very sorry for her at those times. I told her, "you will be seeing me every day whether you like it or not, I will be here." I believe she knew deep down that I would not abandon her no matter how mad she got with me or how hard things got. I had proved that to her several times already. I was there every day as much as my body would allow, but right now after staying with her at the hospital all day, I needed to rest.

I showed up the next day to find Mona talking to a new doctor. She was an Asian lady who was a pain specialist. My son was there and Junior and his girlfriend had showed up as well. Mona was still angry with me and making snide remarks on how I just left her there. I was a little embarrassed and worried the doctor was taking her seriously. She seemed to understand though. I could tell this lady had dealt with this kind of situation more than once.

The doctor asked Mona questions, including about her "living will" and we suggested her son as the executor. The doctor asked about putting me on there and Mona gave a snicker, making it look to the doctor that she didn't trust me, so I said, "Put her son on it." I was sort of relieved not to have that responsibility on my shoulders.

DR. ANGEL

The doctor shocked us all after she did the diagnoses on Mona. She said that the cause of all the pain, swelling and confusion Mona had been having, was not from the actual cancer or what we all assumed was from bone deterioration but simply from "too much pain medication." She went on to say, "too much pain medicine can actually cause more pain." What?! I was in shock as we all were!! I questioned why the doctors at the cancer hospital didn't tell us this or figure this out. She didn't answer me at first and then she said, "The doctor we were seeing at the cancer hospital was her colleague." The doctor told Mona she was cutting back her medicine from forty or more pills a day, down to eight. I was stunned!! Within two days there was a huge difference in my sister. She was way more alert. The swelling was going down in her legs and feet. What was the most shocking to us all was for the first time in six months she finally had way less pain. Unbelievable!!

My sister was much happier of course as were the rest of us. She was near death when I had brought her to the emergency unit only days before. Needless to say, she wasn't angry with me anymore and I was grateful she was doing better. Five days later we brought her home and she was all smiles. Her pain was being controlled now and she finally had some relief. She was eating and drinking better. She came back home, better than she had been in many months. I called her pain control doctor "our angel," when she said goodbye to Mona in the hallway before we left the hospital. The doctor smiled at that title. I cannot express how many doctors we saw with my sister and none of them would say that it was the medication that was killing her slowly and actually causing her to suffer the severe pain, not the cancer. How could this be? They have to be aware? Dr. Angel was! People need to be aware of this because I believe it happens more than we know.

We were the ones giving her medication that was prescribed and slowly overdosing her with them. None of us are in the medical field. We had no idea that the over prescribed pills were what was putting her in so much more pain and causing so many side effects, the swelling, the confusion and sometimes coma like state. The over medicating was what had been causing her to have excruciating pain for months. I am still astounded by this! Mona could have easily died from this and we would never have known the difference. Be aware of this with your loved ones! My family and I are so grateful to Dr. Angel.

    Mona was back to her normal self within a week. Her mind was clear now, she was not dozing off constantly all day and up all night, lost and confused. The constant crying in pain for months had stopped completely. The swelling went away in her legs and feet. She had more energy. It was like a miracle to me. I felt like the old Mona was back. She would have died from an overdose and we would have thought it was from the cancer. That was a huge learning day for all of us and I hope this information might help another family who is going through the same thing. If you recognize these symptoms in your loved one, don't be afraid to question everything. Mona being able to sleep through the night was huge, not only for her but for us as a family. We could now sleep without worrying about her getting up and hurting herself or going outside and getting lost! For the next three months, she was much better than she had been the last six months. She still only ate a little and would only get weaker over time but she had some comfort and quality back to her life. March, April and May would be a lot easier on all of us and I was grateful to have my sister in my life for a little longer and we could now share some quality time together that wasn't filled with stress and pain.

My sister loved for someone to brush her hair and she loved getting a pedicure. Some of the things I was happy to do for her, to give her a small amount of pleasure. Now that she was feeling much better we could hopefully enjoy life a little more together. Every day was precious to us. Mona's feet were very cracked and dry so I asked her one day "would you like a pedicure?" I have always taken care of my own feet and I am pretty good at it. I loved to pamper her and after all she had just been through, she deserved it. I was pleased that she said "I would love one." She lay back in her lazy boy and I went to work. She was totally relaxed in those rare moments. When the home nurse came by for a visit Mona was very happy and proud to show off her smooth feet with her newly painted toe nails. The home nurse lit up noticing the huge difference in my sister. Mona was also much kinder towards me and she was no longer negative about life in general. It was these times that bonded us like never before.

Chapter Twenty-Seven
The Ticking Clock

I would worry about Mona anytime I had to leave her alone, even though she was feeling better and as much as everyone was helping, she was not as strong as before. There were times she would have to be left alone. Her son had gone back to Fort McMurray by the end of March, so we would miss his help. I tried sleeping at her place but it was just too uncomfortable for my body and she couldn't climb the stairs to my place. She insisted she would be okay to stay alone at night, so I had to take the risk to get some rest myself. She did okay for a few weeks and it was a good break for us both. I stayed with her every day until 9 or 10 at night, and then I would go upstairs to my own place. Mona was alert in those days and was sleeping well at night. I was only a staircase away if she needed me. I knew it was only a matter of time before we would need someone to spend the nights with her again. We had asked for help from home care several times before but they would only do home visits.

    We made sure she was all set up before I left every night. We had her medication in order and she was prepared for bed. We made sure she always had the phone next to her. It was hard for me to rest until after a couple of nights and I saw that she was doing okay on her own. My daughter Hanna stepped up to the plate when my nephew left and was showing up every day and started staying many nights when needed as Mona got weaker, as did my son Jesse.

There were a few friends that came to see her and that was always a joy for us. Breda Kavanagh came to visit and as always there was lots of laughter. My close friend Cathy Francis came and of course Mona's best friend and our family friend, Theresa Mcleod, came to visit every few weeks. She stayed a night and Mona was thrilled by that. Mona's daughter would drop by with her baby. That always made Mona happy!

Thankfully home care was coming in once a week and checking on her. There was one lady in particular that Mona and I really liked. I don't remember her name but she had a beautiful, loving soul, and she would take her time in helping us with whatever we needed. I would cry whenever I was alone talking to this lady. It was a much needed release for me. Her compassion was appreciated.

By the middle of May, Mona had dropped a glass on the kitchen floor twice while getting a glass of water. She rarely had to do it herself because I would make sure she had everything in place before I left her apartment. This happened while I was out getting groceries for us. When I got back, thankfully she had got hold of Junior. He was there cleaning it up. She got very mad at him when he said "She is getting too weak to even hold a glass." Not what she wanted to hear! A few days later she did it again. She said "it just slipped out of my hand." She had lost 50 pounds by now and was barely eating a morsel of food again. She inevitably had to get even weaker. Her skin had turned to a greyish, yellow color. I was starting to see some of the signs come back that she was going downhill again. The weakness was the first one. I also knew this was not caused from the medication this time. This was because she wasn't eating enough to stay strong and the cancer was spreading.

I would have to talk her into bathing herself. Understandably, she just didn't have the energy to get off the couch to do it.

The homecare worker would offer to help her and so would I. She wasn't having any part of it. She would do it herself, but by now she was panting for breath to even go to the washroom that was just a few feet away. We would have to get the oxygen on her for her to sponge bath herself. There was one day that I talked her into letting me get her into the bathtub and I said I would wash her. Give her a nice relaxing bath. She was embarrassed about me seeing her nude. I kept telling her, "Mona, we have the same bodies. There is no reason to be embarrassed. You can cover yourself with a towel." She finally agreed one afternoon after bugging her enough. I ran the water and got her oxygen hooked up to her. I couldn't get her to relax at all. I had hoped that she would sit in the tub and just let me to gently sponge her down. No way! She managed to kneel in the tub and I couldn't even get her to sit. She splashed herself down a couple of times and she was out. She was panicking and her breathing was erratic! I wrapped her in a towel, got her back on the couch and calmed her down. I knew we wouldn't be doing that again. So we stuck to what we always did for now, I washed her hair in the sink and she would continue to sponge bath. It wasn't worth stressing her out like that.

A few weeks before Mona went into the hospital for the last time, she started to be up more at night again and now she was starting to get her medication mixed up. I would have them in order on the table with a note for the times to take them. Now I noticed she was taking them at the wrong times. I then got her a pill organizer, marking the time on the lids for her and we tried that, she still took them wrong. I then bought her a wind up alarm clock to try and help her take the pills on time. I decided to wind it up and try it out when I brought it to her place. I got Mona to set the time and alarm while we were there to make sure it worked. Mona fell asleep on the couch and Hanna and I were watching

THE TICKING CLOCK

TV. I didn't realize how loud the alarm would be when it went off. When it suddenly did, the loud clanging filled the room! Mona suddenly sat straight up on the couch and looked straight at us. I still laugh now as I am remembering this. It may seem mean but you had to be there. Hanna and I burst into laughter as I grabbed the clock and tried turning off the alarm. Mona's face was priceless and she had a little chuckle too when she realized what made the noise and heard us laughing. I never saw anyone come out of a sleep like that. It was a little humor that we enjoyed, and needed. I still have that clock on my bedroom dresser. It brings an ache in my heart and a smile to my face every time I look at it.

Chapter Twenty-Eight
Palliative Care

The week before Mona went in the hospital in late May 2013, was one of the hardest weeks for me mentally. She was deteriorating again quickly in the last couple of weeks. She was very weak at this point. I knew it wasn't going to be too long before she wouldn't be able to walk more than the few short steps to get to the bathroom. The more I watched her get worse the more stress I felt because I knew I was going to be the one to have to take her to the hospital again, and I felt we both knew, it might be the last time.

Mona's mind was becoming confused again. Her pain was getting worse which meant the doctors would give her stronger medication, which meant more side effects. Any mention of taking her to the hospital to get checked out would end up in tears and she would beg me to keep her home. Then the guilt!!! I wanted to keep her home, but I needed more help. Mona wasn't sleeping again at night. My children couldn't work all day and stay up all night with my sister, as much as they tried. Hanna had started getting migraines because she wasn't well. I had to have sleep to function and control my own pain. Something had to be done!

I finally had no choice but to call the home care nurse. The tears flowed when I called them asking for help. The person I talked to said "I will send a nurse in this evening to check on her." I had called from my apartment and then went down and told Mona that I called the nurse to come check on her. She was angry right away. I said, "I can't keep up with no sleep, and we need extra help. You are getting too weak and you are confused again. I am afraid to leave you alone." She didn't want to hear any of this.

I know she was scared but now it was my own health as well I needed to consider. I was burnt out!

The nurse showed up and did the usual tests asking Mona the same questions off a sheet of paper that they had asked before, to see where she was in memory and clarity. She failed the test. The nurse was wonderful and very patient with her. I sat next to her and silently cried because I knew down deep inside, the time was coming that my sister would not be coming home and I understood her fear. I was also afraid.

The nurse gently suggested to Mona that she thought it was time for her to go to the hospital. My sister said "No, I don't want to go!" The nurse would look at me with tears rolling down my cheeks, I said nothing. After much gentle coaxing she finally got my sister to agree. I was staying out of it as much as I could. I was thinking maybe she won't be as angry at me, if the nurse talks her into going instead of me. Finally she said "Yes, but just to get checked out." The nurse asked me to call the ambulance because Mona was too weak to walk out to the car. There were seven steps as well that she would have to walk down. The nurse instructed me to ask for a silent alarm. I pulled myself together and I made the call and explained what we needed. The operator asked Mona's age and I broke down and handed the nurse the phone. I don't know why that question made me cry, but it did and I couldn't speak. The home care worker took over and gave them all the information. I packed a small suitcase for Mona with everything I thought she might need while she chatted with the care worker.

By the time the ambulance showed up Mona had been in better spirits. Her medication was definitely kicking in and she was suddenly in a light-hearted mood. She was having a great chat with the two paramedics when they arrived. I had called Junior down stairs to let him know she was going to the hospital and he and his girlfriend came to say goodbye before we left.

Mona was joking with the paramedics as they put her in the special chair to take her down the stairs. She was in her pink flowered pajamas, and her favorite taupe color, suede and fluffy slippers. She was asking the men if they were married or not. We were all laughing by the time they got her outside to the ambulance. Mona was failing terribly but trying hard to set one of the medics up with the nurse. It was very funny and lightened the mood. I felt relief, gave her a kiss and told her I would meet her at the hospital.

When I arrived at emergency Mona was waiting to see the doctor. When the doctor arrived, he was very compassionate and Mona seemed to like him. The doctor wanted to keep her in and she reluctantly agreed. There was no doubt her fears had taken over. I could see the anger in her face and I was going to be the scapegoat the minute the doctor left the room. Hanna showed up and that was always a great relief for me to have her there and it was a little more distraction for Mona. The angry remarks were being flung my way from my sister. One minute I could overlook them, the next, they hurt me deeply. I would snap back at her sometimes because of my own frustration and then I would feel bad for it. "I guess this is it for me," she said while glaring at me.

"I hope not but they have to check you out," I replied. She would snicker and laugh at me with such contempt; it made me feel horrible and hard not to take personally. I felt deep compassion for her most times, but there were moments that I felt like leaving her in all her misery. I knew in my heart I would never be able to do that because I loved her and she was my sister, but boy, it was tough some days. I had to see it through, no matter what.

When the assistant finally brought her up to the ward, she was put in a room with three other patients. It was a nightmare!! I would go visit her and have to spend most of the day pacing the halls because there was such a strong scent in the room from one patient getting sick and having accidents in the bed. The strong smell of pine sol mixed with it was too much for my hyper sensitive nose and allergies. Different doctors were in and out and I would sit and listen to the advice they were giving my sister for as long as I could handle the smell. The doctors would have to call Mona's son for any big decision making because he was the executor on her living will.

The pain specialist Dr. Angel, Mona had seen the last time we were there and who we were all so fond of, came to talk to her again and she was as compassionate as ever. She told my sister they would have to give her intravenous now for her medication. They couldn't give her any more strong pills. She suggested the inevitable, "palliative care." I knew that was the last thing my sister wanted to hear. I stayed out of the decision making as much as I could. Mona would have to make the final decision and right now she wasn't having it! I was praying every day for her and for all of us. We all needed strength.

I had a run in with one of the male nurses while she was in this hospital because of his treatment towards my sister. He was saying things to her when no one was around that I found inappropriate. I spoke to the manager on the floor and she said she would talk to him. My son also had a run in with him when I wasn't there the next day, for not giving Mona her pain medication when he said he would. He went for lunch instead and her medication was overdue. Jesse went and found him, she got her meds!

I went in the next morning and my sister was in tears and so depressed. I asked her if something had happened and she said, "it don't matter, I don't want to talk about it!" She wouldn't even look at me she was so mad. I asked her again, "What happened?" Jesse was there already and he was sitting next to her bed. I tried my best to pry it out of her. My sister didn't want us to say anything more to anyone. "I won't say anything, just tell us what happened." I begged her.

The same male nurse, who we seem to be having some issues with, had told his aid to shower my sister that morning. "The aid who showered me was scrubbing my back so hard I was crying out in pain." she finally said through gritted teeth.

The aid kept saying, "Why are you crying?" Mona said she told her, "You're hurting me! I kept asking her to stop scrubbing so hard, but she wouldn't." Mona looked like she had been through hell!! We all knew the pain that she had in her body, especially her back, why would this nurse do that? I knew the male nurse was behind it and I was pissed!! I felt like we were in some crazy movie!

I left the room so angry!! I paced back and forth in the hallway, trying to think. How could I not say anything, seeing my sister lying there like a wounded animal?! She had made me promise not to say anything. I believed because we had spoken against this nurse the day before, it was taken out on Mona by this nurse and his aid. I went to look for him but couldn't see him anywhere and decided it might not be good to say anything while Mona was still in there. I went back to her room and told her, "We have to get you out of here. You have to consider palliative care

Sister." I was worried about leaving her there for anther moment alone. After seeing the way Donna had been treated at another hospital after open heart surgery, I couldn't believe we were experiencing this kind of treatment again.

My children and I each took turns staying with her from morning to night. My son was there early in the morning before her bath time the next day. I knew that sad excuse for a nurse and his aid would not try anything with him there. My son Jesse is a big man with a compassionate heart who loved his Aunt dearly. He could intimidate the devil himself if needed and I never worried about Mona when he was with her. Hanna and I were there every day until late. No one could spend the night on that ward. There just wasn't room. It gave me strength to have my children there with us.

Mona's youngest son from out of town had showed up for a visit with his girlfriend and her granddaughter which brought her a lot of joy. Her daughter also came to visit with her baby a few times that week. Mona always loved to see them no matter how sick she was.

By day six, my sister had enough of the ward she was on, and after talking to the doctors, she decided to go to palliative care. They were sending her to the one close to the hospital. She was relieved she was getting out of there, but she was still angry she could not go home. She was not impressed at all when I had told her the care center looked like a hotel. I had gone online and researched the center. I just wanted her safe and out of that hospital, I didn't care if she was mad about it at this point. The center also allowed family to spend the night. I knew she would like that.

Mona was taken to the senior's care facility across the road from the hospital. It was very close to my home and convenient for us all to spend every day with her. My son would be there every morning and I would go at lunch time and stay until late evening. Hanna would stay at night. That was the plan. Jesse was with her when they moved her and called me to say "We are at the new place and she is settled in." I was glad he was with her because I knew she would not be mad at my son. They were very close and he was very patient with her. When I arrived there it was like walking into a nice hotel and my sister was sitting up in bed with a smile as broad as sunshine and happy as a lark. I couldn't believe the transformation!

The room was big and private with a big bathroom and everything she needed. It was on the ground floor and was so relaxed and quiet. There was a small modern kitchen and lounge just outside her room. There was a more private lounge just down the hall. It was wonderful. The big windows were right next to her bed and she had a great view of the lawns and a huge tree just outside the window, where two jack rabbits were running around and playing. I sat in a chair near the window, closed my eyes and whispered, "Thank you Jesus." It was everything I had hoped for and more. Mona's happiness would soon wear off but it was good to be in that moment and to see her smile. She would have the proper care, 24/7. It was a huge relief for me! The thing I wouldn't let myself think about was why she was here and what "palliative care" meant. Mona would not forget why she was there when the thrill of the moment soon wore off.

Mona rarely saw her immediate family after this time. There was a lot that happened and that is between them, my sister and God. I am glad Mona's family was there when they were. We all got through it, but not without scars. I believe in giving credit where credit is due, no matter who it is and I believe I have done my best in doing that throughout this book. No matter what I write, people will find fault in it and that's okay. I hope they are at least grateful I kept this at a minimum. There would be many questions as to why Mona's family was not around much in those last months and weeks, I needed to at least address it. There is no learning to be had in denial. Only when there is acceptance is there learning. I leave everyone in as much as they were there. That seemed fair to me. I do send them all blessings to heal and be well!

Chapter Twenty-Nine
Painful Fall

When Mona first went into the palliative care unit, although she was weak, she could walk the short distance to the bathroom with a little assistance, but by week two she started having problems. Her strength was leaving her body quickly. One evening just after supper, the nurse had come in the room to assist Mona to the bathroom. She assisted her with a chair that had wheels on the bottom of the legs, that she would wheel into the bathroom and then help her onto the toilet. The nurse then left the room and told Mona she would be right back. The door was half way open to the bathroom and I walked by it to step outside into the hallway. I suddenly heard my sister cry out. I rushed to the bathroom and saw her lying on the floor, her nightgown up around her and two nurses rushing by me at the same time. I froze and stared down at my sister looking up at me so helpless. I was stunned and devastated to see her like that. I was in the way of the nurses doing their job so I went outside with wobbly legs, and sat in a chair by her door as the nurses helped her in this chair lift to get her back into bed. She was crying out from pain as they lifted her. The tears poured down my face as I sat there feeling helpless. One of the nurses rushed back and forth grabbing things off the cart that was always located outside my sister's door. She looked at me and asked if I was okay. I couldn't speak. I just nodded yes to indicate that I was. I felt heartbroken for my sister! It was so pitiful to see. I felt useless in that moment.

After they got Mona settled back into bed, I could hear her crying, something about her hand. She was high from the shot they had just given her before the fall and was reacting as a small child would. I went back inside the room to see her and I saw right away she had a gash on the back of her hand. It was about two inches long. My legs went weak. Her hand was under her as she fell. The skin was torn back to the bone. Mona didn't seem to feel any pain where the gash was, no doubt because she had her shots just before this all occurred. She was drunkenly trying to touch it and the nurses kept telling her not to as they bandaged it. I shook my head and thought to myself, "My God, what next?!" The nurses there were good to her. After they left and she settled down, I asked her what happened and if she tried to get up and walk before the fall. She said, "No, I just tried to adjust myself on the seat." She had calmed down by then, but I had not, I could feel my insides still shaking. I couldn't get the picture out of my mind of her lying on the floor looking up at me helpless. I knew there would be a change to follow, because she was now too weak to even be left by herself on the toilet anymore. She looked at me and said, "What's next, a catheter?" There it was, the venom back in her tone, as if it were my fault that this was all happening. Sure enough, when I went back the next day she had a catheter. My heart ached for her at that moment, even with the daggers being thrown my way with her eyes. Although it was necessary, I know anyone who sees a family member end up like this must feel the same way. I can't even imagine how Mona felt. She had my sympathy and compassion, times ten!

Every day for almost six full weeks my sister begged and pleaded for me to bring her home. I walked around like a zombie sometimes trying to figure out how I could do it, but there just wasn't enough help. I went over it a million times in my mind.

The guilt I felt was overwhelming sometimes. I knew I couldn't be up with her day and night by myself taking care of her, even with my kids help. If we were rich, it would have been a whole different story to tell I am sure. I'm not sure I will ever get over the guilt of not being able to take care of her full time at home like she wanted. I do know I did the best I could.

Mona would have days when she was more settled and content if she knew someone was staying the night with her. There were two nights my nieces spent the night with her and even that was helpful. The nights that she had to spend alone in her room without family with her were not until the last week she was there. I would pray to God every night, to please let me be with her when she passed and to not let her die alone. That was so important to both of us. Important for her because she was scared and for me because I wanted to be there for her so she wouldn't be scared and so we would get to say goodbye. I wasn't there when Donna passed and I already knew how that felt. I had been very upset about that. I needed that closure. I would be very upset if I wasn't with Mona.

All her anger was coming from her fear and I understood it most days. It was also coming from the heartache she was feeling because she wanted her immediate family members with her. There were days when my sister would cry out, asking for her family who wasn't around. These times ripped me in half and angered me. There were other times she begged for the thing she feared the most, death!! "PLEEAASE," she begged, "PLEASE, SOMEBODY KILL ME, I DON'T WANT TO BE HERE ANY-MORE!!" Those days were the worst!!!

I would go in every day for the first five weeks and for most of them, if my sister was awake she would sit straight up in the bed and say "Okay, let's go. I'm going home today!" This killed me to the core, every time! And then the debate would start. It was like arguing with a child and we just went around in circles. I would tell her the reasons why I couldn't take care of her at home. It was always the truth. I would be with her alone during the day and I couldn't lift her. I made sure she understood, I really wished I could. She would say she understood. Then two minutes later she would start again. "Okay, I am going home now, take me home!" Then she would fight to swing her legs over the railings on her bed. The nurses kept the railing up since her fall off the toilet. I would constantly get her settled back in bed and wait patiently for her next shot that would make her rest for about twenty minutes to half an hour. The shots were every four hours. Then she would get recharged and it would all start again until the next shot. There were many days like this where it went on all day and then there were some days that she looked defeated and totally depressed in the last two weeks especially. Those were the hardest for me, to watch her heart broken and lifeless. She missed her family and she would talk about them often. She would ask for them and I would make excuses for them so she would not be as hurt. Sometimes I said nothing because I felt there were no good reasons.

Sometimes she was more alert and lucid than others and sometimes I wasn't sure what was going on. I was sitting next to her bed one day and she suddenly said, "Who's that tall girl standing there in the basketball uniform?" as she stared into the space next to me. I suddenly became alert myself and sat straight up in my chair. I asked, "Where?" as I hesitantly turned to look where she was looking.

"Right there," she pointed "right next to you." Of course I could not see anyone standing there. I did have goose bumps on my body from head to toe!

Who am I to say she was seeing things? We were in Palliative care after all, where sadly many people had passed away. While Mona was staying there, I saw the silent ambulance sitting out by the entrance on at least five different occasions. Death was a constant there. There may have been someone who passed on in that very room who had been a basketball player in her lifetime? It was moments like this that made me aware of where we really were. It wasn't a nice hotel as I tried to convince myself and my sister that it was. It was a place where sick people came to die. My sister had been totally aware of that before she ever went there and I can't even imagine how she felt. I became even more aware that day that my combatant, willful, sometimes deflated, loving sister would soon pass as well. It filled my brain and heart night and day from then on.

There were days, especially by the last two weeks where Mona's breathing would become faster and I could tell she was panicking to breathe, even in her sleep. She had the oxygen tubes in her nose 24/7. Mona would pull it out of her nostrils when she was sleeping, frustrated with it. I would lean in close to her when she slept restlessly and try and calm her down by whispering to her that "it's okay, you can relax." Just to let her know someone was there with her. Sometimes I would whisper to her that "you are going to be okay and happy, no more pain, no more heartache." I felt we were at a point that I could try and take some of her fear of death away. Her eyes would be closed but I could tell she was listening. "Mom, Donna and our grandmothers are waiting for you." I would describe heaven to her as I believe it to be. I would tell her to imagine, the flowing rivers with the light flickering on them from the warm sun. There were beautiful, vibrant, colorful flowers everywhere in sight; big oak trees swaying in a soft breeze and we would all be together playing with our dolls under a tree, like when we were kids. I would talk about the peace and happiness she would find there. I knew she was listening and letting her imagination go there with me. I would notice her breathing would slow down, she would become more peaceful and she would rest more calmly, until the next time. She was so afraid. I was grateful to be there for her at those moments and I felt good that I was doing something that made her feel better, even for a moment.

I completely broke down only one time in front of her in all those weeks before our last day together. I was sitting close to her and suddenly burst into tears. I told her I didn't know how I would live with both her and Donna gone. It was all too much for me. Who would I talk to? I sobbed and she comforted me, patting my arm gently. There it was, sisterly love....how would I live without it? The last thing I wanted to do was upset her more, but it seemed she felt good about my little meltdown. I know some of her anger came from her feeling like no one really cared about her. If it made her feel better for me to have a meltdown, I was glad it happened. Many times when I sat alone watching her sleep, silent tears would fall. Those were the times so many memories of our life as a family flooded into my brain. Loneliness was something I had struggled with often and it was only getting lonelier as each important person left my life. It seemed my family was getting smaller every time I turned around. I also had fears that I was constantly pushing away. Being alone in the world was one of them. I had made her a promise to stay with her until the end, and I had to keep it, no matter what!

Other times Mona would wake in a panic. Her breathing would become fast and she would grab her sheets and pull on her night gown to try and pull it off to catch a breath of air in her tattered lungs. I would stay calm in those moments and again whisper to her to relax and tell her again about how she would soon be in a beautiful place with our sister Donna, our mother and our grandmothers, who loved her so much. I would describe the blue rivers, rippling streams. The smell of the beautiful flowers and lilac trees everywhere you look. Again, her eyes would stay closed and she would calm down and her breathing would slow down. I could see her physically relax and drift back to a calmer sleep. This went on just about every day in the last few weeks. She fought to the bitter end, with every bit of strength her worn out body had left. Stronger than a Lion!

Chapter Thirty
Musical Therapy

One of my fondest memories with Mona was when Hanna was staying with her for the night. Hanna had her cell phone with her. I asked her if she could play a song for Mona that I had been listening to earlier in that day on YouTube. The song was by the group "Abba," called "I Have a Dream." It was a song my sisters and I loved as young women and in better times. Hanna laid the phone next to Mona's head on the pillow and it was one of the few times since she had been in the care center, that I saw a broad smile come across her face. She relaxed totally into the bed, closed her eyes and sang along quietly, remembering every word. She was already in heaven at that moment. I could see it on her face. Total bliss was written all over her. Music is the one thing that brings us to another place in time, even at our worse times. It was incredible to watch!

    There was a lady on the ward that mentioned there was a cd player in another room we could use if we wanted. We both said it would be nice. She dropped it off at Mona's room the next day. When I got there I turned it on to a country radio station that Mona liked. I said, "I will have to bring in some cd's from home." She liked that idea. A thought came to my mind that I didn't have a cd at home of her favorite singer, Dolly Parton. I went to the mall that evening and hunted down a cd of Dolly's hit songs. I was so excited and couldn't wait to get back to the center for her to hear it. I brought it back to her room and put it on for her that same evening. I didn't tell her who it was, I wanted to surprise her. As soon as it started playing and Dolly's voice came over the small speakers, Mona was all smiles, laying there listening and tapping her foot along with every song that played. "Oh yes," she said. Her head lay back and her eyes closed humming and singing along quietly as I sat next to her. I quietly sang along too and watched the joy happening. In those moments my heart sang too. These moments were the most rewarding and happiest for both of us because they were so few, like the pedicures, brushing her hair for her, brushing her teeth, rubbing her back, holding her hand in quiet moments, these small efforts made her happy. Musical therapy is high on my list for things you can do for your ailing loved ones, and for yourself.

One night I had just got home from being with her all day. Hanna was staying the night with her. Mona had asked Hanna to call me on her phone right after I left. Mona was in a panic because her call button wasn't working. I found out later that they unplugged it sometimes because she was constantly calling the nurses when we weren't there. She was so upset about it. I had to go back over to calm her down. Hanna told me when I got there that she was going to go get the nurse to see if the call bell could be fixed but Aunt Mona would panic and say "No, they will send you home." Mona had forgotten that family could stay with her overnight. After we got her settled down, I left to go home again. Hanna was having a chuckle over how her Aunt was telling her to pretend to be sleeping when the nurses came in so they wouldn't send her home. The drugs would make her loopy and paranoid sometimes, but there was not one time right up to her death that she didn't know who we were.

Mona's best friend Theresa was God sent. She came from Fort McMurray for a full week with our nephew Daniel. It was just two weeks before Mona passed. It was great not only for Mona, but for me as well. I loved having someone to chat with and pass the time while Mona slept. I didn't feel as rushed every day to get over to the Center as soon as I woke up. Theresa and Daniel were always there in the mornings and I would go after lunch. I knew she was in good hands. It was special for us to have them there with us.

Our long time family friends, Janet and Sandy Bursey, came to visit around that time as well. They have been family friends since our high school days in Gander Bay. They brought so much joy and laughter to her room, even though Mona never had the strength to interact as much as she would have liked, she knew they were there and that's what really mattered. Donna's family all came from Fort McMurray to visit her for a weekend. Mona loved them all so much and I was so happy to see any family come around because I knew it made her feel good. Donna's youngest daughter Layla came back the following weekend as well. It was a five hour drive to come visit, so it was very much appreciated.

Our niece Hillire, drove from Calgary a few times to visit her Aunt Mona. One day in particular she drove the three hour trip one way, to sit with Mona for two hours and then drove home again that night. I was so impressed that she did that, but not surprised. She has a heart of gold.

Mona's son Kenny went to visit her one day near the end when he and his fiancé came from Fort McMurray to clean out her apartment. Something I was grateful for that took a burden off me. They were both working in Fort McMurray at the time. When I arrived at the center that day, the first thing I noticed was a huge arrangement of roses and pink flowers sitting on the window ledge, along with the other flowers from family and friends. They were beautiful!! Mona was alone and asleep. I read the card and saw they were from Kenny and his family. I woke her and showed her the flowers and she was very pleased. She loved them! I was very happy he did that. It was a healing gesture that I am sure made a difference to how they both felt in the end. They had been through a lot.

He dropped by to say goodbye to her in the afternoon. They had finished cleaning out the apartment and were on their way back to Fort McMurray. It was very sad to see him saying goodbye to his Mom. I know his relationship with his Mom was complicated and troubled and I also know they loved each other. I will always appreciate the three months her son had spent here with us. We shared many sad times and many good times as a family.

The week before Mona passed I called our father so he could speak to her for what would have been the last time. They both said their goodbyes and I love you. Mona was starting to mumble a lot as she became weaker and I knew pretty soon she wouldn't be able to talk to him at all. Mona fell back asleep after the call but I am certain my father shed some tears.

Chapter Thirty-One
The White Lie
―――――――――――

On the fifth week of Mona's stay in palliative care, I walked into her room one day to find her lying in her bed half nude. Her blanket covered her to her shoulders. I could see she had finally got her hospital gown off that she had fought with constantly. Thankfully, someone had gone in her room and covered her with her blanket. She had started trying to rip her hospital gown off many times over the last few weeks. I got her to wear her own gowns a few times but that didn't work either. It was harder for the nurses to deal with her changing's and intravenous when she wore her own gowns. The nurse told me one day my sister was pulling at her gown to try and breathe better. I had figured that much watching her.

Her door had been ajar, so anyone walking down the hallway could have seen in her room. I wondered how long she had been lying there in her nakedness before someone went in to cover her up. These were the things that bothered me most about having to leave her alone when I would go home at night. As good as the nurses were, some days I would only see them every few hours when it was time to give Mona her shots and they would check to see if she needed changing. Many times I went to get them when she did. That always worried me. I went to her bed and sat by her making sure that she stayed covered up until she woke up. When she woke I said, "Mona, you took your gown off, you can't do that okay?" She just motioned "yes" seeming unaware of what had happened. I got another gown and put it on her. My sister with so much pride would be devastated to know anyone had seen her like that. I knew the nurses and aids were very busy, and they definitely needed more staff like most of our care centers. Seeing a loved one this way feels like someone reaches in your chest and squeezes your heart. Nobody should ever have to see the people they love end up this way, but the reality is many of us will end up being taken care of the very same way. We are all going to die, there's no getting away from that. Those of us that go in peace when we are hopefully older, with family around us and very little pain and sickness are blessed, and so are our families.

  By the last week Mona was in palliative care, neither of my kids could stay with her at night anymore because of their jobs. They would come every evening and stay with me and my sister when they got off work. My son had started a new job and was working early mornings. He had already spent many nights staying with his beloved Aunt but now he couldn't. Mona looked in his eyes one evening when he was sitting next to her and she asked him, "Who is staying with me tonight?" My son just looked at me and then lowered his head. I know it killed him, and he didn't answer. I spoke up and said, "He can't Mona, he is working early in the morning. You will be okay. The nurses know to call me if there is a problem. I can be here in 5 minutes." We all knew how scared she was and we were all doing our very best. She didn't have the strength to be angry anymore but you could see that constant fear in her eyes. I prayed every night that she wouldn't die alone. "Please God, let me be with her," I pleaded every night before I slept. I had to have faith and constantly remind myself to stay positive. God had our back and so did our guardian angels.

Mona's breathing was becoming more erratic. She was gasping for breath in those final days, panicking sometimes to get air into her lungs. Every time her doctor would come to check on her she was usually sleeping. By the last week he looked at me and said, "It's tough hey?" I just nodded my head, to answer "yes." I couldn't speak about anything without getting emotional at this point. He said "she could go on like this for days or weeks. There is no way to really measure someone's fight and strength." Mona had already gone past his first prediction by two weeks and I could tell he was being cautious in what he said. Mona had fought like nobody I have ever known. For someone who had not cared much about life when she first came to Edmonton almost two years earlier, it was something to watch her kicking and screaming all the way until that final week, with the little strength she had left in her.

Mona had not been drinking anything, barely more than a few sips of water a day for weeks. She was eating nothing at all by the last week. Her skin had turned even more greyish, yellow now. Everything she said was a low whisper. Before I went home at night I would leave the music playing low in the CD player to keep her company. Most nights I was in so much pain I was awake until four or five o'clock, sometimes seven in the morning. I slept in as long as I could which meant I didn't get back to the clinic some days until after lunch. I did my best to be there by noon or one o'clock at the latest. I knew Mona would be waiting for me. I would wake up and rush to get back to her. I had the same routine every day, eat breakfast or lunch, get showered, dressed and out the door, always afraid of what I would face when I got there. Keeping my anxiety under control was something I had to work on every day. I would usually try and grab a book and read something positive before I left. "Just get through today" was my mantra every morning. Jesse and Hanna were my biggest source of strength that last week and I am thankful they were there. Other than that, we saw no one else in the final week of my sister's life.

Sister was sleeping a lot but there were still days when she would want to sit up in bed and she would fight to try and stay awake. She would doze off within two minutes after she sat up.

I asked her one of those very bad days when I didn't know if she would make it through the day or not, if she had seen our sister Donna around? She just said "no" and left it at that. I really felt in my heart that our sister Donna would come to get Mona when it was time. No one could tell me different. I knew that would give me and Mona some kind of comfort and I prayed and hoped somehow when Donna did come, that I would know she was there.

The days and evenings were long when I was there alone. I started bringing a book to read the last few days and I would sit in the lazy boy next to her and try and read as she slept. Her breathing was raspy and shallow by now. I could hear the fluid in her lungs making gurgling sounds as she slept.

We constantly brought fresh cups of water filled with ice to try and get her to sip a little water. Most times now the ice just melted and formed sweat on the outside of the clear, plastic cup, not being touched.

The day before my sister's passing; her breathing was so bad you could hear the gurgling of fluids very clearly from inside her heaving chest. Hanna sat there across from me and we would look at each other and I would just shake my head. I didn't think my sister could hang on much longer. This made me even more afraid to leave her. Hanna stayed with me as long as she could and then I hung on until 10 pm that night. It was draining for the healthiest person to watch. I took her hand and asked one more time if she wanted to see a Minister, she firmly shook her head "NO," I said "okay." I don't know if I did the right thing by following her wishes at this point but I did.

When we were alone that day, I told my sister a white lie. I felt certain she was still fighting and hanging on, trying to stay alive until she saw her family. Although I tried to feel compassion towards them most days because I knew it was a lot for them to handle and I felt some anger towards them other times, but I had to think about my sister's feelings first. Not my own and not theirs. They were not devils by any means. They were family that Mona and I both loved who had their own issues. I had to forgive them all somewhere along the way but more importantly, I wanted my sister to before she passed. I knew I would eventually because the last thing I would do to myself was keep my anger bottled up inside or hold grudges. I had learned how to deal with my own feelings when I needed to. Most of all I had to forgive myself somewhere along the way for being so angry with them.

To lie to my sister would be a challenge for me. At least she would not be looking me in the eye because I could never do it if she was. I stood at her bed, took her hand and leaned in close to her. I spoke to her as gentle as I could and whispered, "Sister?" She lifted her head off the pillow a little and mumbled the word "what." I said, "Dad and Junior, I named all her children, one by one, can't come to see you. It's too hard for them to see you like this. They wanted me to tell you they all love you very much." I realized at that very moment, the lie I thought I was telling my sister was really the truth. They didn't ask me to tell her but I did know they probably would have wanted me to say what I did. She had been listening intently! I saw relief on her face right away. She whispered back to me in one raspy breath, "Tell them I love them too." And her head went back to her pillow. I squeezed her hand and whispered, "I will." By then the tears were streaming down my face. For the first time through all we had been through, I saw the look of total peace on my sister's face. I left her room to let her sleep and I went out to the lounge area, flopped in a chair, covered my face with my hands and I sobbed quietly. "Forgive me God." I whispered. Going through something like this for the first time, you have to learn as you go on what to do. There is no right or wrong. I seem to go with my instinct in the moment. Treat her how I would want to be treated. We all do the best we can. I was feeling a great release knowing that my sister would not die thinking that her family didn't care about her because I knew they did and for once, I felt like I had done something right without questioning myself. I did it for her, myself and maybe them as well, and I don't regret it. I never lied to my sisters in my life, and I felt I just might be forgiven for this one.

When I left later that night, I kissed her like I always did and told her I loved her and would see her tomorrow. She gently shook her head and whispered in her weak and muffled voice, "okay, love you too." By then she didn't ask any more if anyone was staying, she was too sick and weak to even care. With a heavy heart, and legs that felt like rubber, I walked out of the Center that night to go home and I felt her time was very near!

Chapter Thirty-Two

Her Last Breath

I hardly slept that night, dreading what was inevitably coming. I couldn't get my mind to shut off at all. Surviving it all without having a breakdown was a big concern for me. I didn't know how much more I could handle. I do believe everybody has their limits and mine was way past what I ever dreamed I could do. I had absolutely no strength left. My arms and shoulders were weighted down and painful, built up from carrying such a heavy load of stress and worry over the past year. Mona could fight this for weeks for all I knew but how could I hang on?! I prayed every night that God would give me strength to see it through until the very end. I knew somewhere deep down I wouldn't give up, even if I ended up in a wheelchair, I would be there. Keeping my promise was important to me!

I woke up at 11 a.m. after having been awake until 7am. I had an overwhelming feeling of not wanting to go back there that day. I remember feeling, I'm done!!!I pushed myself to keep moving, ate breakfast, showered and sat at the table to try and put on a little makeup. When I looked at myself in the mirror, the exhaustion and sadness I saw, no amount of makeup would hide. I kept thinking I have nothing left! I felt it in every part of my body and soul. There was plenty of self-talk going on in my brain that morning. "You can do this, just put one foot in front of the other and keep moving." I took my time and got ready. Maybe I was more hesitant to go because I also knew what was coming. I was not prepared for it to be today though. I was in denial, not wanting to face it. How are we ever really prepared to lose a loved one?!

I arrived at the center at 1:30 p.m. I could feel my legs wanting to collapse from under me but I just pushed myself to keep walking into the front lobby, down the hall, turn left through double doors, turn right, and straight down the hall. When I walked into Sister's room, I was shocked at how much worse her breathing was, just overnight. She was alone in her room. I walked over to her bed and felt myself wanting to just collapse right next to her. Death was looking me in face and I was terrified!!!

The whole top half of her body was now jerking with every breath she took. She was lying on her right side with her right hand tucked under her cheek. Her eyes were closed but the left one was open just a little. She didn't know I was there until I spoke. My heart was breaking in two, watching her whole being struggle for every breath. Everything I was feeling came to the surface in that moment. Then I broke!!!

"Sister, this is enough....you have to go now." I spurted out quietly between sobs. Just like that!! I couldn't believe these words were coming out of my own mouth. Tears were streaming down my face. I felt sick to my stomach. She tried to reach her hand to me right away to comfort me, but she didn't have the strength. I took her hand and continued...."You fought a long hard battle and you did well, but this is enough! I can't come here anymore, I'm done!" She was nodding her head in agreement. For the first time I could see, she was ready to go. "You have to go now," I pleaded again. "If you see Mom or Donna, I want you to take their hand and go with them, okay?" I was wiping the tears from my face as I spoke, they were pouring down. I could not hide my grief from her. She nodded her head again, "yes." There was a nurse in the room with us now and she came to the bedside to adjust something on the wall behind me and she placed her hand on my back, a gesture of comfort for me that I appreciated at that moment. I asked my sister if she wanted me to pray with her and she nodded, "yes."

I said the Lord's Prayer that we had said so many times together as children. She tried to mumble part of it but there were no real words at all now, just a raspy sound coming from her. I asked her, to ask God to forgive her sins and she nodded "yes." Then I asked her if she accepted God into her heart and she nodded her head "yes." I felt really good that we had done that together. I felt so grateful and so sad at that same moment, and the tears kept flowing. I know I am not a minister, but at least it was something spiritual before she passed. It gave me and her some kind of comfort. I sat next to her, held her hand and put my head down and quietly begged God to take her today, over and over in my head, while the tears streamed down my face. I asked Donna to come and get her so she wouldn't be afraid and I prayed for the strength for myself, to survive losing her.

For the next three and a half hours, I left her room often because her harsh breathing was taking any life I had left, out of me. Every five or ten minutes she would wrap her arms around her bended knee and try and pull her leg up towards her body. I think she would do this because it was the only way she could get any breath into her now, fluid filled lungs.

I would go to the kitchen area right across from her room or I would stroll down the hallway to the lounge that was cozy and vacant. There were a lot of books there that I would pick up and browse through without reading a word. My heart was gripped with pain. I didn't know how I would ever be mentally healthy again after all this. It was too much!! I thought about calling Hanna but I knew she and Jeanna were with their dad who was in town visiting and they were going for a late Father's Day meal. I still had no idea if Mona would hang on like this for a few more days. My son Jesse was at work. I knew Jason would have been there if he lived closer. So I sat and then walked and I waited. I believe as everything in life, I was meant to be alone with my sister those final hours. If anyone else was there with us I maybe would have been less focused on thinking of the things I needed to say and do with her.

I went back to Mona's room and sat by her bed. Suddenly she pulled her hand away from her cheek and waved towards the ceiling and she smiled. I was stunned!!! Then she raised her left arm and reached straight up in the air, trying to grasp something with her hand. I watched in amazement!! The fact she could even raise her arm like that was shocking to me! Goose bumps suddenly covered my body! "Sister, is somebody here?" I asked. She tried to say something but I couldn't pick it out. I leaned closer to her and asked her to repeat it several times but couldn't understand the mumbling, so I left it alone. I was frustrated now. I wanted to understand every word she tried to say to me. I had a feeling someone was there, and my feeling was that it was our sister Donna.

I whispered to my oldest sibling, by ten and a half months, that she would be at peace soon, no more pain. She was going to that beautiful place with the flowing rivers, fields filled with beautiful flowers, big oak trees everywhere you look and the warm sun on her face. She seemed to relax a little more with every beautiful description I could imagine to tell her. I was so grateful at that moment to be there with her and able to give her some comfort. It meant everything to me and I am certain it did to her too. She wasn't mad at me anymore.

I decided after about twenty minutes to go back down to the lounge and take another break for a few minutes. I was never in the lounge any longer than five minutes and I would make my way back to her room. I was restless and weak. My own body was wracked in pain from top to bottom. I ignored it. The words, "I can do this" playing over and over in my head. I was sitting next to her again when she suddenly started to try and say something to me. I listened but couldn't pick it out. "Sister, I can't understand, please say it again." I said patiently. She let out another breath of air with a mumbling that I could make no sense of. I wasn't giving up, I knew it had to be important for her to even try and talk to me. She didn't have any strength left but she was still very aware I was there. I asked her again to repeat it, "Try one word at a time," I said, and she did. The first raspy word I understood. I repeated it back to her, "Donna?"

"Yes," she whispered and nodded. I felt every hair on my body rise and I froze. The next line floored me! "She's here to get me," she let out in one quick raspy breath. I repeated it back to her to make sure I was hearing her right and she whispered, "Yes," and again nodded her head.

I cried, "You go with her okay?!" She nodded her head "yes." I felt so many emotions flood through me all at once. I felt comfort, peace, and the deepest sadness that I was losing another sister. I was elated that our sister Donna had come to take her, and yet I felt devastated because I knew the end was coming. It was a true roller coaster ride of emotions! I went back to the hallway and leaned my back to a wall to hold me up and to try and breathe. I suddenly couldn't seem to breathe! I still had no idea how long she would hang on, the nurses hadn't said anything to me when they went back and forth in her room and I was afraid to ask. It was still a guessing game for me, but at least now I knew my other sister, my soul mate was there with us. I talked to her in my head. "I know you're here with us Donna, help me too if you can," I begged. I thought about calling my daughter again but then I thought, she would be here soon.

When I went back to her room and walked in a few minutes later, I noticed Mona's breathing had suddenly changed. She wasn't taking long raspy breaths anymore. Her breathing was fast, quick breaths now and her body wasn't jerking back and forth like it had been. I went to the other side of her bed and sat there watching her, comforting her and letting her know I was there. I held her hand and smoothed her hair. The nurse had come in twice while I was there to give Mona another needle. There were two nurses back and forth with us that day, one was a nurse named Ella and the other nurse was named Lilly who had been giving Mona her shots. They were both close to my age and very kind. Just after I had returned to the room, Ella came in and when she looked at my sister she said, "Oh my." She seemed startled. She came to my sister's bedside right away and took her pulse, which was something I never saw them do. I kept thinking at this point that there was no death, her spirit would live on. The thought that she would soon be rejoicing with our family members in the spirit world was comforting to me. I was there when my mom passed away but so was the whole family. This was certainly nothing like when my mother had passed. I knew from weeks before in talking to the head nurse that when the breathing suddenly changes and becomes quicker, death was coming. "This could go on for minutes or days" she said. I believed in my heart that Donna was there to take her home soon. An assistant and the other nurse Lilly came into the room at that moment and Ella looked at them and said, "Let's turn her over."

I moved back and went to the end of the bed. I felt I was in the way of the three of them doing their job so I said, "I'll just go to the lounge." I walked down the hall to the lounge, sat down and I had just picked up a book when I heard someone running in the hallway. I looked up and Ella was at the door. "Come quick," she said, "She's going!" My heart raced as I jumped up and tried to run behind her but my legs wouldn't let me. "I have to phone my daughter!" I said. She pointed to the phone on a table and I quickly picked up the phone dialed the number with shaky hands and my daughter answered. I said "Come now, Aunt Mona is going." She replied, "Okay." I hung up the receiver and rushed to her room.

I walked in the room and my sister was lying flat on her back in the bed, the blankets pulled up neatly to her chest and her hands crossed and folded on her chest. I went to her and covered her hands with mine, her eyes were open and she was taking her last breaths calmly and peacefully. In that moment I thought about all her heartbreak and now in this moment, it was all over. I lowered my head down and kissed her face over and over and told her over and over we loved her and would miss her. "Your family loves you," I said again and again! By now there was only air coming out of her lungs. Her eyes looked straight ahead, not moving. I knew she was gone. I looked at the ceiling and repeated over and over that I loved her. Lilly left the room several times but Ella stayed on the opposite side of the bed from me and she was struggling when I looked at her. She said, "I lost my brother two days ago." There was an instant connection and I reached over and took her hand and said "I'm sorry," as I squeezed her hand. Tears were streaming down my face and I could see Ella was struggling to stay strong. I asked her "Is she gone?" because there were still a few low breaths coming out but nothing going in. She checked her eyes and closed them, she said yes, and there were no more breaths. I laid my head on my sister's chest and wept. I heard footsteps running and I stood up. It was my Hanna and her boyfriend who had spent so many days with us. She looked at the bed at her Aunt and then she looked in my eyes and we just hung onto each other and cried! Jesse walked in a few minutes later and said his goodbye. We held hands and walked out of her room, down the hall, turn left through the double doors, turn right to the main lobby and out into the warm, sunny day!

RIP Sister, I love you!

Mona, 2004

Chapter Thirty-Three
Goodbye Kiss

I left the Care Center and went home, walking under that cloud again that now felt so familiar to me. I had to make the necessary phone calls. I wanted to be left alone in my grief and I was exhausted. I called my father, my aunts, Jason, Mona's best friend Theresa, and a few other family members. A few hours later after I knew everyone was called that needed to be, I made a post on social media to all the family and friends that had been a constant source of support for me and my family over that last year. Some were close school friends of Mona's and mine. I thanked the people that had been there for us to the end. I got back lash later for that because I didn't thank the people who had left her heartbroken. I am sorry for that, but I wasn't up to doing that right after I just watched her take her last breath without any of them being there. I knew the rest of the family had all been called and notified. Everyone else was free to make their own announcements. That's how I felt at the time.

    I felt that fainting feeling again that evening and the feeling of floating. I knew it was anxiety. I kept telling myself positive affirmations. "I will get through this." I whispered to myself. "This too will pass," was repeated multiple times in my head. Every time I repeated those words I felt relief, even just for a few moments. I was well aware I was walking a thin line. Then there would suddenly be an uncontrollable flood of grief. It would suddenly hit me and could have me on my knees in a second! I let myself feel it all when I was alone. I also had a sense of relief that my sister was finally out of her misery and I was thankful I managed to keep my word to her!

I could feel Mona was around me. Her energy was near, I knew that. It may have been both her and Donna for all I knew. I had a long night of worrying about my father and what he must have been feeling. Dad seemed to handle it okay when I called him. I knew he was expecting the call and was staying strong for me, but I could only imagine how he was after we hung up. Dad and Mona were very close. He told me when we had an open heart talk two years after Mona passed, that losing Mona was the hardest for him and I understood that knowing their connection.

I believe it is much harder for families to accept losing a loved one when it happens suddenly and unexpected. I believe having time to accept that a loss is coming helps us more because we have time hopefully, to at least say our goodbyes. I do know most of us are not getting out of here without experiencing one or the other. Like many, I have experienced both with my family. I think the shock of losing a loved one suddenly may hit us harder initially, but to watch them suffer for a long time just to have them around longer seems selfish to me, and yet understandable, because we don't want to let them go. It is not easy either way!

I finally closed my eyes around four o'clock in the morning. I could feel she was with me. I would tell myself to not to be afraid, it was my sister, she would protect me now. Just as I closed my eyes and finally got comfortable, I felt a pressure right in the center of my forehead, like someone gently pressed their thumb on my forehead. I remember opening my eyes and wondering, "What the heck?" and then realizing and believing, "she just kissed my forehead." That made me smile. I whispered "thank you sister," and went to sleep.

The next night scared me a little more. It was around the same time 4am that I started to doze off again and suddenly there was a loud noise in the room that made me sit straight up in a split second. My heart was racing a mile a minute. I had goose bumps from head to toe! The light was off in the bedroom, with just the hallway light on. I looked all around and could see nothing had been disturbed to make such a loud noise. Then I looked up at the window just 5 feet in front of me and I thought. "Wow!!!!" The hair stood straight up on my arms! I had pull blinds on all my windows, underneath the curtains. I have had them for the ten years, ever since I lived in this apartment block. In all that time and even after this one incident, this has never happened again. I could never get this blind to go all the way up to the top of the window as many times as I tried, it would only go three quarters of the way up and there it was, right to the top of the window! I had pulled the blind all the way down about an hour before. The sound it made told me it flew up at a very high speed. I was stunned, scared and a little thrilled!!

My heart was still speeding minutes later and I continued to take slow breaths to calm myself down. "Okay," I said to my sister after a few minutes, "You are definitely here with me Sister and you obviously don't want me to go to sleep, but you can't do this. Don't scare me like that please." I talk to my sisters like they are still around me, because I do believe they are always with me, especially when I need them. "Go downstairs and visit Junior," I said with a grin. I started to relax after about an hour and finally went to sleep without another incident since that night. I carry you and our journey together forever in my words and in my heart Sister!

Mona was cremated and her memorial service was held here in Edmonton two weeks after her passing.

Chapter Thirty-Four

Angels Among Us

I believe they surround us in our darkest hours, they protect us and love us. They are our angels!

On August 14,th 2014, just over one year after Mona passed, I was watching music videos on YouTube, when something triggered me to suddenly type in the headline "Videos of Angels." I clicked on search and all these videos came up of what was believed to be "angels caught on videos." I was immediately fascinated by this. I am a believer in angels, I always have been. I never knew that these videos had existed. I was glued to the computer screen for the next three hours. Some of the videos were obviously questionable, but there were others that were amazing to watch.

As I was watching the videos of the many angel sightings, the memory came to me of the reading I had one year before, almost to the day after Mona passed. Paul's words to me were, "She's watching out for you and she says 'thank you'." I remember smiling at the thought while watching the videos. I was thinking of my sisters, my friend and my mom the whole time I watched the videos. It gave me comfort to think of them all as angels now. I finally turned off the computer around 1 a.m. and fell asleep. I had been concerned about my finances for the past month because I was struggling. I have learned through positive reading, to push those worries away and just have faith! I had even more faith after watching the videos and thinking of my loved ones watching over me.

I woke up that morning, went to the bathroom, and then to the kitchen to put the kettle on to boil water for my morning tea. The videos from the early morning were still fresh in my memory. As I passed the entryway in my apartment, I noticed something out of the corner of my eye. I looked down on the floor and saw that someone had slid an envelope under my apartment door. I stopped in my tracks and thought, "weird." I had Christmas cards sometimes pushed under my door from my neighbors, but this was August month. I picked up the card sized white envelope and peeled it open. I pulled out the contents. It was a cheque that had a piece of paper wrapped around it with a note attached. It read, "Cash this today, paid in full!" I looked at the cheque and nearly fell over. It was for $5,000. It turned out that it was money that was owed to my sister before she passed away. She had told Junior a few months before her passing that she wanted her money to go to me. I told her repeatedly, I didn't want it. Thirteen months after her death, here it was. I felt very grateful and very emotional for a while after that happened. It was clear that my sisters are my angels and watching over me. To me, it was a very special gift from heaven from my sister that she would want me to keep and for that reason for once in my life, I kept it. Thank you Sister! That would not be the only gift she sent me!

Chapter Thirty-Five
New Beginnings and Steve

Six weeks before Mona went into palliative care, I was at her apartment and we were watching our favorite TV show, Family Feud. I was sitting on the couch and she was laid back in her lazy boy chair looking comfortable in her cozy flannel pajamas. She had her favorite cream colored, fluffy blanket covering her. Steve Harvey was our favorite TV host and we watched him daily. He made us laugh a lot which was much needed and good therapy for both of us.

My sister was in a good mood that day and was feeling pretty relaxed. I could tell she was a little high after just taking her meds. Remember, my sister did not like alluding to her death at all, so I was quite surprised by what came out of her mouth at that moment. My family and I couldn't even get her to talk about funeral arrangements. She was in denial and she was scared, which was understandable. None of us ever pushed her to talk about it.

Out of the blue she said, "I'm going to find you a man, someone to take care of you." I knew what she meant right away and was taken aback by the comment. I knew she worried about me being alone after she was gone. She knew how much I suffered with the pain from fibromyalgia because she experienced it too. She was a "worrier" by trade. I went along with her scenario. Who am I to say if she could create a small miracle for me or not after she left our world?!

"Well, that would be nice." I replied. "If you can do it, I would like someone like Steve Harvey. Someone who is funny. He doesn't have to be perfect, just perfect for me."

"Alright, if I can I will." she said.

After a short pause I asked, "But how will I know if it's the right man? I will need a sign."

"I don't know." She replied and we both thought about it for a minute.

"I know, maybe his name will be Steve?" I said jokingly.

My sister and I got a chuckle out of that and she said, "Yes, wouldn't that be something. I will try my best." I put it in the back of my mind with a smile and the thought, "I won't be surprised if it happens." Five minutes later the conversation had left my mind and I didn't think of it again. This was in April 2013 and my sister passed away three months later.

On September 11, 2014, seventeen months later, I was going out to a country club here in Edmonton. It was a club I went to three or four times a year when my friends played there. I arrived there close to 9 p.m., stepped out of my car and stood by the entrance. I was looking in my purse for my lip balm and then I looked up. In the distance about fifty feet away I saw a man strolling through the parking lot, hands in his pockets, head looking down at the ground as he walked. I could tell right away he was a deep thinker. "Well now, who is this I wonder?" was my first thought. It was like I recognized him and I couldn't stop staring. He was a slender man, mixed color hair, dressed in black jeans, a black long-sleeved shirt, and black cowboy boots. He looked up and saw me at that same moment and the both of us locked eyes from the distance and we continued to keep them locked as he walked towards me and as he passed by me. He continued to walk towards the other end of the parking lot and he turned away. There was a row of cars parked between us. "What the heck is wrong with me?" I asked myself. I had never stared someone down like this in my life! I felt it was rude but I couldn't stop myself. I had met plenty of men in my life that I was attracted to but not once did I behave like this. I might smile at them, hold their gaze for two seconds and then look away, I was too shy and I blushed too easily to hold a glance any longer when first meeting someone. I felt I suddenly had no control at all, it was crazy! I wanted to look away but couldn't. I saw the words "Security" written on the back of his shirt as he walked past me. I thought, "This is interesting, in all the years I came to this club they never had security here before." As he walked away from me, he turned his head looking back towards me and we both continued to stare. I felt like I was in the "Twilight Zone." It was certainly a new experience for me and it was intense! He disappeared around the back of the club and I went inside.

I sat where I normally sit and pretty soon my friends showed up. The security guy was now inside the club walking past my table, several times. (grins) He would also sit on a stool in the corner not far from where I sat. The staring continued. I really felt like I knew him. We didn't talk that night other than to say "Hi, how are you?" when he passed me by as I stood outside with my friend on a break. I said, "Fine thanks, and you?" He said, "Fine thank you" and he walked on. I could feel the intense attraction to him across the room all night and I believed he felt it with me as well.

The very next night I was going out with my daughter Hanna for dinner to meet a man she had wanted me to meet for a few months. She was going to University at the time and she also worked part time at a pub in St. Albert. She kept talking about this group of men that would frequent the pub, most of them married but there was one man my age that was single, funny, rich, and "sort of attractive," according to her. Apparently she had told him about me and he wanted to meet me as well. Whether someone is attractive or not is a matter of one's own taste and opinion. "He owns a big home and drives an Audi," she had mentioned a few times. Anyone that knows me well knows I don't care about those things but I finally agreed that I would go meet him. The fact that she thought he was funny and attractive intrigued me, so I went. I had been alone for many years now and I knew my kids wanted me to find someone.

I had a lot of fun that night as I sat at the pub with my daughter and "the guys," but I knew right away I was not attracted to "Mr. Rich" although he was sort of funny. When we left the pub I said to my daughter, "Thanks, but he's not for me dear. Take me home to get my car please. There was a security guy I saw last night at the club. I want to go meet him tonight if he is there." I felt intrigued to find out more about the "mystery man."

When I arrived at the club sure enough, he was there again. I felt my heart race a little when I saw him. I felt the butterflies as well. I had not felt that way about anyone for a very long time. I thought, "I am not going to be sitting here all night again and not talk to this man. I need to be brave and make a move." Something I had never done in the twenty years that I have been single was approach a man I didn't know. As he walked past my table I nodded my head to motion him to come to me. Even though he was walking away from me, I knew he could see me in his peripheral vision. Sure enough, he walked over to my table and I said something I never thought in a million years I would ever say to a man, "Do I know you from somewhere?" My very next thought was, "Kill me now!!!" The oldest line in the book often used by men, and the words just slid out of my mouth like the snakes I detested. The crazy thing was I wasn't feeding him a line. I really felt like I knew him. "I used to come here about two years ago," he replied. I knew I never saw him there before, I would have remembered. "No, I don't remember seeing you here." I said. He admitted a long time after that he felt he knew me as well when we met. He was leaning in very close to me to talk and the eye contact was incredible. The attraction was off the charts! To find this at my age was amazing. One thing that I always found attractive in a man was a cleft chin and this man had one. He also had a smooth British accent, which was unexpected and sexy. The band started playing and he waved and walked away.

When the band took their break I went outside with one of the band members and while we were standing there chatting, the door pushed open and out came the "security man" to join us. As he stood with us, we did the introductions. I held my hand out and said, "I'm Diane, this is my friend Del." He reached out to shake my hand and simply said "Steve."

We all started to chat and the conversation was flowing. The funny thing was, Del would ask Steve a question about where he was from and Steve kept looking me in the eyes when he answered him. It was all I could do not to laugh out loud and I was a little embarrassed by it. It felt like the two of us were in our own space. I was smitten and the connection I felt was instant. I was confident he was feeling it too. We couldn't take our eyes off each other. We talked at every break that night. I found out Steve was born in Oxford, England, moved with his family to Portsmouth when he was nine and was raised there. He joined the British Air Force in his earlier years. He had also been a former fireman for many years, and then he became an HSE (safety) officer. He had been working in that field in the more recent years. He was doing the security work for his brother-in-law who managed the night club and hotel while he was waiting to go back to work in his field. Things had become really slow in Alberta at this time. "I am not happy doing this and the pay sucks but it is a job." he said. I didn't really care if he dug ditches, but he has a lot of pride and I could tell it bothered him. I went out three more nights within the next two weeks to see him and it was a blast getting to know him.

Two weeks after I met Steve it was my birthday, September 25th. I was sitting at home that afternoon watching TV when I suddenly had a flashback about a conversation I had with Mona a few months before she passed away. I suddenly remembered her telling me "she was going to find me a man." The spark of the memory made me focus on remembering more of the conversation with her. Because I couldn't remember anything else right away, I almost pushed it aside but something wouldn't let me. The more I concentrated, the more parts of the conversation were coming back to me slowly, word for word. It took an hour or so to remember the whole conversation and the part about the name I had chosen to let me know if it was the right man she sent, came to my mind last! My whole body was covered in goose bumps when the name "Steve" popped into my mind and I remembered saying it to my sister! I thought, "This cannot be possible?!!!" I was flabbergasted!! This was beyond incredible, especially since I seemed to be falling head over heels in love with this man already and had felt such a strong, soul connection with him right away. It was undeniable!! The fact that the memory came back to me on my birthday was also unbelievable! A message no doubt, that she kept her promise and this was my very special gift from her. It is crazy and makes me laugh just writing this but it is completely true. I remembered thinking "I wouldn't be surprised that it would happen" and believing it was possible was the great part. Even though things have happened often for me by simply believing, it is still always a surprise when it does. It is the law of the universe!

I went out for my birthday that night. Steve remembered it was my birthday which was surprising to me. I had mentioned it to him once briefly the week before. We were going for his breaks together by now and the conversations were none stop, as was the flirting. He was fun and very charming. When we went to go back inside the club and he grabbed the door handle to open the door for me, he turned around and kissed me three times. It was sweet, tender and stirred up feelings inside me that I had not felt for many years. I fell in love with my "twin soul" at that very moment. When I drove out of the parking lot that night I was so excited I took my hands off the steering wheel, threw them up in the air and said, "Thank you sister, thank you!"

There was Steve Harvey, and now there was "My Steve." I referenced that title to him many times since then. The best thing about it all was that I was falling in love with him before any of these synchronicities ever happened. There were many different things that would make me stop in my tracks over the next twenty-three months. My Steve's last name was also very close to the spelling of Steve Harvey's...both had six letters, the last three the same.

I did not tell him about the conversation with my sister until six months after I met him and we were at my apartment. We were relaxing, sipping wine and I decided to tell him. I was a little scared of what he might think. Steve is not a big believer in spirituality as I am and when I finally told him, it did leave him a little speechless. He was a believer at one time he told me but something had changed him. I think deep down, he still believes.

I believe we are "a match made in heaven" literally! I also believe we were brought together to help each other learn and grow.

The more I got to know Steve, the more similarities I saw. I often felt from the very beginning, that I recognized myself in him in many ways. Our facial expressions and reactions are the same. It took months before I noticed we both have a matching ingrown mole on the side of our noses. The similarities became clearer to me over time. He brought my silly side out, which is a first for me. I had never been that way with anyone in my life. We share the same humor, blush easily and we share a lot of the same loves, like movies, music and food. I have never met another man that likes the "romance comedies" as much as I do. He might kill me for saying that (grin). We are very forgiving, affectionate, and flirty. We love to share a wink across the room, and his favorite tea biscuits in the world are mine too. It is my own recipe.

He is very quirky at times, which I love. He makes me laugh out loud often. I've had some great belly laughs thanks to him and what's even cooler is I make him laugh. We are both a little naughty, which is always fun. I often have referred to him as a cross between John Cleese and Roger Moore. John Cleese is my favorite British actor/comedian and I had a huge crush on Roger Moore when I was a young woman. Steve is very intelligent and witty and we have had great conversations about many topics. Our social skills are the same. We both love having conversations and fun in small groups. Music is a big thing with us and he has a wonderful singing voice and has played drums in the past. We both love to draw, dance, are light sleepers and night hawks. He likes to read and write as well.

As much as we are alike we also have our differences. Steve likes the finer things in life whereas I like nice things but want to keep things simple. We are more alike than different in our goals and we are both very good at sitting and talking things out. I am more willing to jump in with two feet when I feel something is right. Steve is more analytical and has to think things through. I go by what I feel. When I feel something is right, I don't like to waste time. I believe that comes from losing most of my family members so young. He can be stubborn, admittedly so. The sweet thing is when he finally admits to it. I love when someone admits their own flaws. We both are sensitive and can be temperamental, but we calm each other down quickly. In the end, I believe we balance each other out.

Steve and I have both expressed our love for each other. I said to my sister in our conversation, "he didn't have to be perfect" and he is not and neither am I. However, I do believe "he is perfect for me," and we are good for each other. He makes me feel protected and safe whenever I am around him. The first time he said the words "I love you" to me was very surprising and sweet. He was about to walk away after we kissed goodnight and I was about to close the door to my vehicle. I heard him mumble, "love you" under his breath. It didn't register with me for a second but when it did, I grabbed his coat and pulled him back and said "WHAT?" several times before he answered. He had a big grin on his face. We both laughed and he kissed me again and repeated, "I love you." I said, "I love you too." As I drove away, you couldn't wipe the smile off my face if you tried. I was elated!

On March 2nd 2015, my daughter was visiting me at my apartment. We had been through a rough weekend with her and our family losing her Pomeranian dog named Dixie. She was in our family for twelve years. She was very much loved and she would be greatly missed. I felt terrible for my daughter. Hanna was sitting on my sofa and I was close to her sitting in my lazy boy chair knitting a scarf. We had been talking about our weekend and how rough it had been. Then Hanna asked me how Steve and I were doing? Suddenly, for no apparent reason I started to cry. I was sobbing uncontrollably. Hanna was shocked and so was I by this sudden flood of emotions. Hanna looked on in disbelief! "Mom, what's wrong?" she asked. I put my hands in the air making the gesture that "I don't know." I felt heartbroken the rest of the day and although I was sad about losing Dixie, I instinctively knew, this was something deeper. As soon as she said Steve's name, I fell apart. I didn't understand it because Steve and I were in a good place. I wasn't worried about anything.

The next night I went out to the club to see Steve and was surprised he wasn't working. I asked one of the waitresses if he was coming in and she said, "No, he is going to B.C with his sister, his Mom passed away." She had just heard this. I was surprised and heartbroken for him! I couldn't just go to see him because he had been staying with his sister. I went home and called him right away. He answered and the first thing he said was, "my Mom died." I felt like crying, he sounded so sad. I said, "I know darling, I am so sorry." He went on to tell me "she passed away yesterday and wasn't found until today." I realized the sudden grief I had felt the day before had probably been around the same time his mom passed away. It was a sign letting me know something sad was happening to someone I was connected to and loved.

Steve's mom was in my dreams that night, although I had not met her. He had brought her to a gathering in my dream and I looked at her and told her she looked lovely. She was eighty-eight years old when she passed away but in the dream she looked in her late fifties. Her hair was a light auburn color. She was slender and was dressed elegantly. For the rest of the week while Steve was away, I felt his grief many times. I was happy when he finally returned and I got to wrap my arms around his neck and hug him tight. His skin looked a little grey and I could see he had been

NEW BEGINNINGS AND STEVE

through a lot. My heart broke for him and his family. I knew how it felt to lose your Mom. RIP Margaret!

It was over three years before I met Steve that I had my first reading with the psychic Paul at "The Russian Tea Room," here in Edmonton. I have the reading saved on a tape. It was about eight months after I met Steve that my son called me up one day and wanted me to listen to the copy of his reading he had with Paul. Yes, my family has all gone to see this wonderful psychic, at least once. There was something specific my son wanted to know from his reading that was important to him at that moment. I had four different tapes in my drawer, one belonged to Hanna and there was one for Jeanna as well as mine and my son's. I wasn't sure which was which so I put the first one I took out into the recorder and I hit play. I did not rewind it. The tape was already half way through the reading. It didn't matter; I just wanted to see who's reading it was. Paul was speaking when it played. I listened carefully. It was the tape from my reading over three years before and he was describing a man I was going to meet. "A romantic interest," he said. Right away I remembered being told I was going to meet my "twin soul mate" by a lady psychic who had been there before my reading with Paul. I suddenly remembered how this lady's face lit up when she said that to me. I let the tape play on. Pretty soon I could not believe what I was hearing.

Paul was giving me a description of this "romantic interest" I had coming to me in my future. He said, "I would be meeting a man with mixed color hair, a slender man and he saw the word 'security' written on his back." My mouth dropped open! He said "I also see suspenders but I am not sure what it means." My first thought at the time of the reading was a, "firefighter." They wear suspenders. I even mentioned it to Mona and Hanna after the reading that I believed it was a firefighter Paul was talking about. He went on to say, "There would be an emotional connection and he was a major card for me." He said, "This man is a little rough around the edges and I would love his mind. Being with him is like playing a game of chess." He went on to say that "he is intelligent and he is much more grounded than my last relationship. You will be a good match and this relationship would take months, it was not a rush job. The only negative would be this man would be more focused on his work and less on romance in the beginning." This is all so true. I was floored by the insight! I believe the reason my son called that day and asked me to listen to his tape was so I could actually hear my own reading from back at that time. I never would have remembered a word of it on my own and there were times I needed a little reassurance when things weren't moving as fast as I would have liked with me and Steve.

  I have some fears that still creep in on me once in a while and I needed the reminder that I am on the right track and there is really nothing to fear besides my own thoughts. These fears and insecurities come from so many let downs in my life in my long term relationships before this. I struggle with trusting people sometimes. My biggest fear was to lose Steve and I knew I had to work on that. I felt Steve had many of his own fears to overcome as well. I instinctively knew he had been through a lot in his lifetime and for those reasons was holding back from me as well. As positive as I try and live my life, I am not perfect in being that way all the time. I kept the notes I had written that day and later told Steve about the reading but I left out one part that hasn't happened yet. I will tell him when it does.

  This was a forty-five minute tape that I played by chance, three and a half years after a reading and it had started playing in the exact spot where Paul was talking about the one man he saw in my future. I think it was the perfect time that I really needed to hear this.

NEW BEGINNINGS AND STEVE

I won't talk about all the synchronicities between Steve and I but I feel I do have to mention the ones where Steve Harvey was involved because they are incredible! I had mentioned in the first chapter, after the break-in into my apartment that I read Steve Harvey's book "Act Like A Success, Think Like A Successs." It took me about a month to finish reading that book, only because it was hard for me to focus after the burglary and I wanted to take my time reading it so I would be able to absorb what I was reading. I feel that book got me back on track after such a stressful time in my life. Not only because of the burglary but also losing my dad so soon after it. The book had been sitting on my coffee table for about a week, waiting for me to get the time to pick it up and read that last chapter. Steve Harvey gives some wonderful advice on how to reach our goals in life and be successful at finding out what our gifts are and using them to our benefit. I needed this book badly at that time, especially after having my computer stolen with my book on it. One quiet night I picked up Steve's book and finished reading that final chapter. At the end of the final chapter Steve Harvey talks about his family, mentioning his children. I thought "it is strange he didn't mention his wife at the end as well." Anybody who knows anything about Steve Harvey would know how much he loves his wife. I decided to go to the front of the book and read the acknowledgements to see if he mentioned her there. He did talk about her throughout the book a few times. He always talked about her with great love and respect. The moment I went to turn the pages to go to the front of the book, the thought entered my mind, "wouldn't it have been something if his wife had the same first name as mine as well." Now what would ever make me think that at that very moment? It had never entered my mind before. I thought it was a little strange to even have the thought. I believe it was my intuition or my sister whispering to me that I needed to pay attention at that moment. I may have needed a little reminder at the time that solidified that meeting my Steve was no coincidence.

I couldn't remember what Steve Harvey's wife's name was but I did know it wasn't "Diane." So why would I even think that??? Sure enough, there in the front of the book Steve wrote a beautiful paragraph about his mother, father and then his wife. As I read the beautiful messages, I read his wife's name and a switch suddenly came on in my head and then the goose bumps!!! Her first name is "Marjorie!" What I realized in that very moment was, so is mine! Wow!!! It was too much for me to believe, much less anyone else!

I was named after my Grandmother, Maisie Marjorie Peckford. My first name is really Marjorie but somebody decided when I was a baby to call me by my middle name, Diane. I never think of myself as Marjorie. This was brought to my attention years ago when I ordered my birth certificate. When it arrived I was very surprised to see my full name was actually, "Marjorie Diane Waterman." Even writing it that way now feels very strange to me. Again, the chills! "Everything happens for a reason!"

These synchronicities happen a lot with Steve and me. There are too many to ignore. I know he has had them as well. Things that make us stop and pay attention. Steve keeps things more to himself and I am obviously more open. He did approve of this chapter after he read it. He said he was pleased with it and it was accurate, which meant a lot to me.

I do believe we were definitely brought together by my angel/angels. I could imagine Mona and Donna holding hands and dancing with joy when Steve and I first laid eyes on each other and connected. I love the way we look at each other and the way he breaths me in when he nestles his face into my hair.

Meeting Steve has given me hope that there is something more for me in the future. I have told him often, he is my hero. The work he did in his life and in sacrificing his life, as a military man and firefighter, makes him a hero to me. He has spent his whole adult life focused on keeping people safe.

You are my bright light at the end of a very hard road. I don't know what the future holds for us and if nothing else, I hope we can remain lifelong friends. I believe!

The end and the beginning...

Me and Steve. June 2017

About Me

I was born in a beautiful, quiet town in Newfoundland called Gander in 1956. I lived there for 4 years with my family before my father accepted a job in Goose Bay, Labrador where we all moved. We moved back to Newfoundland to a little community called Clarke's Head, Gander Bay where I started High School and we lived there until I was 19 years old. My parents then moved back to Gander in 1976 where they lived out their lives. I married a man from Labrador and moved to Alberta in 1978 where I have resided ever since. I have 4 adult children and 4 grandchildren. I divorced my husband 20 years ago and decided after working in jewelry for 15 years, I needed to slow down after being diagnosed with fibromyalgia in 2011. A year later at 55 years old I found my new love, writing. This is my second book since then. The first one was published in October 2013 called, "When Lilacs Bloom."

www.ingramcontent.com/pod-product-compliance
Lightning Source LLC
Chambersburg PA
CBHW030513080526
44586CB00011B/168